Ancient Peoples and Places

THE
SELJUKS

IN ASIA MINOR

General Editor

DR GLYN DANIEL

Ancient Peoples and Places

THE
SELJUKS
IN ASIA MINOR

Tamara Talbot Rice

80 PHOTOGRAPHS
56 LINE DRAWINGS
AND 2 MAPS

FREDERICK A. PRAEGER
Publisher
New York

THIS IS VOLUME TWENTY IN THE SERIES

Ancient Peoples and Places

GENERAL EDITOR: DR. GLYN DANIEL

BOOKS THAT MATTER *Published in the United States of America*
in 1961 by Frederick A. Praeger, Inc.
Publisher, 64 University Place
New York 3, N.Y.
All rights reserved
Library of Congress Catalog Card Number: 61-13433
© *Tamara Talbot Rice 1961*
Printed in Great Britain
by Western Printing Services, Bristol

CONTENTS

ILLUSTRATIONS

Introduction

IT IS FASCINATING to pause at the crossroads of the past and meditate on the different situations which might have developed had the decisions taken at a particular time been altered or reversed. In the long run it was often the seemingly less important events that determined the course of subsequent history, perhaps many centuries later and perhaps in regions far removed from those in which the events themselves took shape. This has seldom been more true than in the case of the Seljukid Turks. Although their empire endured for little more than two centuries, between A.D. 1071 and 1300, their influence on present-day politics is still apparent, for there is reason to believe that it was the Seljuks' reputation for invincibility (based as it was on the series of great victories which they wrested from the Byzantines, the Crusading forces of Western Europe and the armies of the powerful Shahs of Kwarazm) that prompted the Mongols to attack Kievian Russia instead of concentrating on the invasion of Persia and Iraq. But for this, Russia, even if still partially subjected to the Mongol yoke, might nevertheless have been able to strengthen the ties which she had established with Western Europe, and in that event she might have assimilated something of the quickening spirit of the Renaissance, and shared in Europe's social and economic development. How different might recent history have been, had events fallen out in this manner!

Nor is this all. If history is a compound of chance and character as Herodotus believed, then the Seljuks must be held responsible for another event of major significance to Europe. According to tradition the Turkish tribe of Osman owed its first territorial possessions in Asia Minor to the gratitude of one of the last of the Seljukid sultans of Rum. It was from that small

13

Anatolian foothold that the Osmanlis were later to advance westward, to sweep victoriously over much of Europe, and to found in Constantinople an empire of world-wide significance. What would have been the situation, one asks, had they not been granted a fief by the Seljuks?

The momentous nature of these events did not, however, serve to perpetuate the memory of the Seljuks of Asia Minor. Those historians of the nineteenth and early twentieth centuries who remembered them at all were inclined to belittle them by denying them credit for any positive achievements other than those of a military character, for these writers regarded the Seljuks as a group of semi-nomadic barbarians whose chief claim to notoriety rested on the havoc they caused in Asia Minor. Our generation has learnt that destruction is part and parcel of all forms of warfare. The Seljuks were constantly involved in fighting, and the trail of devastation which marked each engagement bears testimony to their far-flung territorial gains, to their spectacular advances and periodic retreats, as well as to the sudden changes in their policy. At the same time it is now evident that a network of impressive roads, a magnificent series of vast caravanserais or rest-houses, a number of splendid hospitals, seminaries and schools, and numerous mosques and mausolea were established as a result of their concern for the economic and spiritual needs of their people.

The Seljuks were empire builders by instinct, and fate willed it that their rise to power should coincide with an unusually exciting period in history. It was an age of great spiritual and intellectual advancement, of which the development of Benedictine monasticism and the idea underlying the Crusades represent two facets; new economic and social systems were evolving; thought and learning were entering a fresh stage. The world seemed full of great men, and the Seljuks had a striking share of distinguished and able administrators, of inspired poets and profound mystics, of thoughtful philosophers and probing scientists. Malık Shah, Sultan of the Great Seljuks of Persia, himself a writer of quality, had at his side as wise counsellor and loyal servant, one of the most enlightened statesmen of his day, the eminent Nizam al Mulk. Avicenna, Omar Khayyam, Firdausi and Saladin were but some of the great figures who dominated the scene in the East; in the West, spiritual leaders such as St Francis of Assisi and intellectuals such as Frederick II Hohenstaufen helped to establish the cultivated outlook—for Frederick, for all the truculence of his temper, yet remained 'the Wonder of the World'. Betwixt East and West stretched Byzantium, with its wealth and power not yet decimated, its millennial culture still intact, the despoiling chivalry of Chris﹍ tendom having failed to destroy the creative spirit of its people, even after the disaster of the conquest of Constantinople in 1204. Wars, it is true, were practically uninterrupted, and the Seljuks, like all Turks, were basically a warlike people. Yet they knew also how to make good use of the intervals of peace, and it is the story of their accomplishments and of the legacy which they left to their Ottoman followers that is told in this book.

Acknowledgements

I am very grateful to my husband for his unfailing help and to Mr and Mrs Mellaart and to Professor Kurt Erdmann for their generous response to my numerous requests. I should also like to acknowledge my indebtedness to Their Excellencies Mr and Mrs Emel Esin, to the Press Attaché of the Turkish Embassy in London, to the directors of the Ethnographical Museum at Ankara, the Museum of Turkish and Islamic Art at Istanbul, the Konya Museums and the Kayseri Museum, as well as to Mr Koyunoglu of Konya. In addition I should like to thank Miss Serare Yetkin, Mr W. E. D. Allen, Professor Storm Rice, Mr Basil Gray, Mr Pinder Wilson, Miss Gordon and Miss Josephine Powell for help in obtaining photographs, Mrs Ruth Daniel for drawing the maps, Mrs Margaret Scott for drawings for the figures, Dr Walsh and the staff of the libraries of Edinburgh University and the School of Oriental and African Studies for their help in tracing obscure books. I am especially grateful to Professor Celal Esad Arseven, Professor Oktay Aslanapa, Professor Tahsin Ozgüç and Professor Mahmut Akok, as well as Mr Seton Lloyd for permission to reproduce some of their plans; also to Messrs Benn Ltd for permission to quote from E. G. Browne's *Literary History of Persia*, to Luzac and Company for permission to do so from Gibb/Barthold, *Turkestan down to the Mongol Invasion*, to Routledge and Kegan Paul Ltd for allowing me to do the same from *Anna Comnena's Alexiad* and to Bernard Quaritch for permitting me to reproduce some brand marks and quotations from Yacoub Artin Pacha's *Contribution à l'étude du blazon en Orient*. Above all, however, I must express my sincere thanks to the Russell Trust of St Andrew's University, whose generosity enabled me to return to Anatolia to explore some of its ancient caravan routes.

Present-day Turkish spelling has been adopted for the names of all places which formed part of the Seljukid Kingdom of Rum as well as for those situated in Horasan and Central Asia. It has also been used for the names of Seljukid and other Turkish notables and for the monuments in the area, but Persian and Arabic names have been transliterated; thus the Seljukid sovereign's name is spelt Keyhüsrev, whereas the Persian hero's is given as Key Khusraw. Exception has been made in the case of such words as shah, pasha, and the name Seljuk, which have been so widely used in English over so long a period that it has been thought better to retain their traditional spelling. In modern Turkish ç should be pronounced as ch; c as j; ş as sh; ö and ü as in German, and the dotless i, as u in fur.

An oblique stroke is used to separate two dates [e.g. 1077/78] where either of the two Christian years may correspond to a year of the Hegira.

List of Significant Dates

AD   **689**   The Ghuzz entered Transoxania.

         712   The Ghuzz gained control of Central Asia and penetrated to Samarkand.

920–60   The Seljuks became converted to Islam.

     1034   The Seljuks gained control of Horasan and began to regard themselves as the champions of the Abbasid Caliphs.

     1040   Battle of Dandarqan when the Seljuks defeated the Ghaznavids.

     1043   Tügrül made Merv his capital and was recognized as the Champion and Protector of the Caliph, his name being read in the Kutba.

     1045   The Seljuks raided Armenia for the first time.

     1058   Tügrül crowned Sultan of the Eastern and Western worlds by the Abbasid Caliph in Baghdad.

     1071   Battle of Manzikert when the Seljuks defeated the Byzantines.

1077/78   Süleyman became Governor of Rum.

     1078   Süleyman proclaimed himself sovereign and chose Nicaea for his capital.

     1086   Süleyman declared himself independent of the Great Seljuks.

     1134   Konya became the capital of Rum.

     1242   Battle of Kuzadag when the Mongols defeated the Seljuks.

The Seljukid Dynasties

Ancestors of the Seljuks

TUQUQ=Tımuryalık=Paighu=Yabghu.
SELJUK his son; died at the age of 107.
ISRAIL=Paighu Arslan, his elder son, and
Mikail, a younger son.
TÜGRÜL BEG, Çagrı Beg, Ibrahim ibn Inal,
sons of Mikail. Çagrı Beg died in 1061.

The Great Seljuks of Persia, 1037–1157

1037–1063	RUKNÛDDIN ABU TALIB TÜGRÜL.
1063–1072	ADUEDDIN ABU SAÇA ALP ARSLAN.
1072–1092	CELALEDDIN ABUL FATH MALIK SHAH.
1092–1094	NASIREDDIN MAHMUT BARGIYARUK.
1094–1104	RUKNÛDDIN ABUL MUZAFFAR.
1104–1117	MALIK SHAH II and GIYASEDDIN ABUL SAÇA MUHAMMAD.
1117–1157	MÜIZEDDIN ABUL MARIT SENCER.

The Seljuks of Syria

? –1095	TUTUŞ brother of Malık Shah of Persia.
1095–1113	RIDWAN his son, reigned in Aleppo.
1095–1103	DUKAK son of Tutuş, reigned in Damascus.
	ALP ARSLAN and SULTAN SHAH, sons of Rıdwan, reigned for a short time as vassals of Lulu Shah. Their heirs have no bearing on the subject of this book.

The Seljuks of Iraq

1131–1134   MAHMUT proclaimed ruler by Sencer.

1134–1152   MALIK SHAH and MUHAMMAD sons of Mahmut.

1152–1159   SÜLEYMAN their brother.

1159–1175   ARSLAN their uncle.

1175–1194   TÜGRÜL son of Arslan, last sultan of Iraq, killed by a confederate of the Shah of Kwarazm.

The Seljuks of Rum, 1077 to about 1308

? –1064   KUTULMUŞ probably the son of Israil Arslan Yabghu; killed fighting near Rey (now the rendering 'Kutlımış' is sometimes preferred).

1077–1086   SÜLEYMAN his son; killed or committed suicide at his defeat by Tutuş of Syria.

Interregnum

1092–1107   DAVUD or MAHMUD KILIÇARSLAN I Suleyman's son; died by drowning. According to Sarre, he married Isabella, a sister of Raymond St Egidier; he was also married to the daughter of the Emir Tzakas of Smyrna.

1107–1116   MELIK SHAH brother of Kılıçarslan I.

1116–1156   RUKNÛDDIN MESUD I son of Kılıçarslan I.

1156–1188   IZZEDDIN KILIÇARSLAN II son of Mesud I; in 1188 he divided his kingdom between his eleven sons, and perhaps also his daughter. He died in 1192 in the house of his youngest and favourite son, and eventual successor. In his lifetime Ankara was for a time ruled by his brother Shahanshah.

The Division of Rum between Kılıçarslan's Eleven Sons

1 KÜTHÛDDIN MELIK SHAH in Sivas and Aksaray.

2 RUKNÛDDIN SÜLEYMAN SHAH father of Izzeddin Kılıçarslan III, in Tokat and the lands extending towards the Black Sea.

3 MUHÛDDIN MESUD SHAH in Ankara, Çagrı and Eskişehir; his Ankara coins are dated to 1200 and 1202.

4 NÜREDDIN MAHMUT SULTAN SHAH in Kayseri, though it would seem that at one period the old sultan had given this town to his daughter.

5 MÜGISEDDIN TÜGRÜL SHAH father of Ruknûddin Çihanshah and of Ismet Hatun, in Elbistan.

6 MÜISEDDIN KAISER SHAH in Malatya.

7 NASREDDIN BARGIYARUK in Niksar and Koyluhisar.

8 NIZAMÛDDIN ARGUN SHAH in Amasya.

9 SENCER SHAH in Eregli.

10 ARSLAN SHAH in Niğde.

11 GIYASEDDIN KEYHÜSREV I father of Keykâvus I, Keykûbad I and Celaleddin in Keyferidun, Uluburlu, Konya and Kütahya.

1192–1196 GIYASEDDIN KEYHÜSREV I youngest son of Kılıçarslan II.

1196–1203/04 RUKNÛDDIN SÜLEYMAN SHAH his brother; died suddenly five days after killing his brother Muhûddin Mesud Shah of Ankara.

1204– ? IZZEDDIN KILIÇARSLAN III son of Ruknûddin Süleyman Shah.

1204–1210 GIYASEDDIN KEYHÜSREV I resumes power.

1210/11–1219   IZZEDDIN KEYKÂVUS I son of Keyhüsrev I, died of consumption.

1219–1236   ALAEDDIN KEYKÛBAD I brother of Keykâvus I, died by poison, probably ad﹍ministered at the wish of his son, Key﹍hüsrev II.

1236–1246   GIYASEDDIN KEYHÜSREV II married first (1232) the daughter of the Eyyubite Prince of Aleppo, then Russudana, daughter of Queen Tamara of Georgia. Among his children were Keykâvus II, Felekeddin, Kılıçarslan IV and Keykûbad II.

The Triumvirate consisting of Keyhusrev II's Three Sons

1246–1283?   IZZEDDIN KEYKÂVUS II first ruled with his brothers, then singly over territory lying west of the Halys. His children included Melik Konstantin, who became a Christian, Kılıçarslan and Mesud, who accompanied his father to the Crimea.

1246–1264   RUKNÛDDIN KILIÇARSLAN IV father of Keyhüsrev III and of Huand Hatun; ruled first with his brothers, then over territory lying east of the Halys. Died by murder at Akşehir.

1246–1257   ALAEDDIN KEYKÛBAD II died during a mission to the Mongol Court.

1264–1283   GIYASEDDIN KEYHÜSREV III son of Kılı﹍çarslan IV, brought to the throne at the age of three by the Pervane Süleyman Muin ed din; murdered at Erzincan by order of the Mongol Ilkhan Ahmet.

The Mamluks entered Konya in 1277

1283–1298 GIYASEDDIN MESUD II son of Izzeddin Keykâvus II, reigned over lands lying east of the Halys in succession to his nephew, Keyhüsrev III.

1283–1302 ALAEDDIN KEYKÛBAD III son of Faremurz and cousin of Mesud II, reigned over lands lying west of the Halys, but his sovereignty was contested by Mesud III, son of Mesud II, each of the former deposing the other till Keykûbad's death
when

? –1308 GIYASEDDIN, Keykubad III's son, and Mesud III, contested the throne till Mesud's murder by the Mongols.

GIYASEDDIN disappears without leaving a trace and the dynasty ends, though a reputed son of Mesud II,

GAZI CELEBI, may have continued to rule for a time at Kastamonu and Sinop.

The Beylıks which sprang up in Asia Minor after the Collapse of the Seljukid Sultanate of Rum

c. 1300–1403 AYDIN of Birge, Ayasuluk, Tire and Izmir.

c. 1292–1406 ÇANDAR of Kastamonu, Sinop and Safranbolu.

c. ? –1373 DÜLGADIR of Maraş, Antep and Antalya.

c. 1335–1381 ERTENA of Kayseri, Tokat, Sivas and Zile.

c. 1299– ? EGREF of Beyşehir.

c. 1303–1429 GERMIYAN of Kütahya, Ladık, Manisa and Balıkesir.

c. 1300–1426 HAMID of Egirdir, Isparta and Antalya.

c. 1385–1459	ISFENDIYAR of Sinop? and Cankırı.
c. 1256–1483	KARAMAN of Nigde, Ladık?, Laranda (Karaman), Ermenek, Mut, Aksaray, Sivrihisar and Konya.
c. 1380–1425?	MENTEŞE of Aydın and Sultanhisar.
? – ?	RAMAZAN of Adana and Tarsus.
c. 1300–1410	SARUHAN of Manisa, Foça, Saruhan, Gördes and Demirce.
Late 13th century onwards	THE OSMANLIS of Eskişehir, Iznik, Bursa and, ultimately, the whole of Byzantium and the countries which came to comprise the Ottoman Empire.

CHAPTER I

The Background

Months are needed ere, by earth and water fed, the cotton seed
Can provide the martyr's shroud or clothe the fair in raiment fine;
Days are needed ere a handful of wool from back of sheep
Can provide the ass's halter or the hermit's gabardine.
Lives are needed ere by Nature's kindly fostering, the child
Can become a famous poet or a scholar ripe and fine.
> From the *Divan of Sana'i*. Sultan Sencer's period.
> Translated by E. G. Browne.

THOUGH OUR CONCERN is with the Seljuks of Rum, that is, of Eastern Rome—to use the name by which their contemporaries knew them—when they established themselves in Asia Minor after their victory over the Byzantines in 1071 at the battle of Manzikert, it is necessary to begin their story a good deal farther to the east and at a much earlier date. In the 7th century they were one of twenty-four Ghuzz tribes into which, according to the 10th-century Persian geographer Mahmud Kashgari, the Turkish nomads who lived on the borders of Afghanistan were then divided. Some scholars tend to identify these Ghuzz with the Hiung-nu, who as far back as 1200 B.C. had plundered China's western provinces; or with their successors the Hunnu, who were routed by the Chinese in the year A.D. 215, when they fled westward and overran Europe as the Huns.[1] Those of the Ghuzz who remained in Asia multiplied and prospered. At the time of the Arab invasion, that is to say early in the 8th century, they became known as Turks. Apart from the god Umay whom, like the Shamans of a much later date, they revered as the protector of their children, the Turks worshipped the elements; but their sense of nationhood was even then so keen that the Orkhon inscriptions, the earliest

25

written records associated with them, frequently refer to 'the Turkish sky', 'the Turkish earth and water' and so forth.

The Seljuks entered Transoxiana with some of the other Ghuzz tribes in the year A.D. 689, and by 712 they had gained control of western Central Asia and penetrated to Samarkand. Though some of them then adopted semi-sedentary occupations, all continued to live in tents, and they developed the habit of concentrating in and around Samarkand in the summer months and moving to Buhara for the winter. By the 10th century they had become the most vital of the Ghuzz tribes settled on the lower Jaxartes.

SELJUK

The Seljuks claimed to be of royal descent, tracing their ancestry back to Seljuk who, according to the *Tarıhı Güzide* or *History of Mustaufi*,[2] belonged to the Kabak tribe of the princely house of Afrasiab. Many legends are associated with Seljuk's name. One of these tells of his encounter in single combat with the khan of the powerful Jewish Khazars,[3] but the 11th-century historian ibn al Athir ascribes this combat instead to Tuquq—also known as Tımuryalık or 'Iron Bow' —whom he identifies as Seljuk's father. Whilst contemporary scholars discount this story, al Athir regards Tuquq as the true founder of the dynasty, partly because he was also called Paighu, a name which Dunlop[4] defines as a corruption of the title '*Yabghu*'. According to ibn Habreus, another early Islamic historian, Tuquq began his career in the army of the khan of the Jewish Khazars, the two peoples having been connected by trade for already quite some time.[5] He rose to the rank of commander, but died while still a young man, when his son Seljuk was scarcely more than an infant. The Khazar ruler took pity on the orphaned prince and, placing him under his personal protection, he arranged for the boy to become a member of his household, and to be educated at his court. The young prince does not appear to have been grateful for these benefits, for the

Khan's wife overheard him speaking disrespectfully of his protector. Angered by Seljuk's words, the Queen complained to
her husband, who contented himself with banishing the offen-
der from his kingdom. Seljuk returned to his own people to
find that fighting had broken out between their Iranian suzerains, the Samanids,[6] and the Turkish tribe of the Karakhanid.
Quick to take advantage of the trouble, he led his people into
Djand, which was still under Samanid control, and refused to
withdraw till his tribe had been freed from paying the Samanids
a tribute which Seljuk believed to have been unjustly imposed
upon them. He died at Djand at the age of 107.

Seljuk's four sons and successors, Mikail, Yunus, Musa and   RELIGION
Israil, strengthened their hold on Buhara and Samarkand. The
choice of Jewish names for two of these princes seems to confirm Dunlop's suggestion[7] that Seljuk, together with some of
his courtiers, may well have followed the Khazars who had
befriended his father in becoming converts to Judaism; but
some Russian scholars regard it as an indication that the Seljuks
had adopted Christianity as their religion. The question is a
difficult one to resolve, largely because the Ghuzz as a whole
had become the prey of missionaries of various sorts from a
very early date. The Buddhists had been the first to enter the
field, penetrating into Central Asia from India in the 3rd
century A.D., when they began by using the Hindu alphabet
for their texts, but soon abandoned it for the Soghdian or early
Persian. The Manicheans were the next to reach the Ghuzz,
and the Christians followed soon after. It is probable that each
of these made converts among various sections of the nomadic
population, but the Christians never acquired great influence
among them, and even the Buddhist ascendancy proved short-
lived, ceding to the Sasanian which, in its turn, was replaced
in the 7th and 8th centuries by that of the Arab traders, who
were entering Central Asia in ever-increasing numbers with

the object of reaching China. Though their presence in Central Asia put a term to Persian predominance, they were not at first able to affect the religious outlook of the Ghuzz, the majority of whom appear to have been Shamans.[8] Nevertheless, the regular increase in their number gradually began to make itself felt, and by the middle of the 9th century the larger cities of the Oxus had to provide mosques for the Arab community. The Ghuzz thus developed an awareness of Islam, and, by the end of the 10th century, probably some time between 920 and 960, the Seljuks had become ardent converts of Muhammad.

ISRAIL

Israil was to prove a great general and leader of men. In 1003 he went to the assistance of the Samanids who were once more at war with the Karakhanid; he emerged from the conflict with the right to use certain grazing grounds situated in Horasan, that is to say in Samanid territory. The arrangement was condoned by Mahmud of Ghazna, though by 1025 the latter had become so apprehensive of the Seljuks that he decided to enter Israil's territory, hoping that a display of strength might curb the rising tide of Seljukid imperialism. His forebodings increased on hearing Israil say that he could summon a hundred thousand men to arms merely by sending an arrow from his quiver round his people, and that he could double the number if he sent his bow.[9] Mahmud accepted the remark at its face value, but he refused to follow the advice of his counsellors that he should amputate the thumbs of all male Seljuks so that none of them should be able to draw a bow. Instead, he contented himself with admonishing the Seljuks and taking one of Israil's brothers back to Ghazna, where he imprisoned him in his great fortress of Kalanjar. It may have been this that decided Israil to cross the Oxus and invade Ghaznavid territory.

The combatants were not so very unequally matched, so that although the Ghaznavids eventually succeeded in stemming the nomads' advance, capturing both Israil and one of his sons, the peace proved no more than a respite. The enmity of the Seljuks was aggravated by the Samanid Shah's decision to withdraw the grazing concessions which his predecessor had granted to the Seljuks, a measure which strengthened the nomads' determination to acquire sovereign powers for them/ selves.

The leadership of the tribe passed to Israil's brother Mikail, who established himself in Buhara. In 1029 he and his three sons, Tügrül Beg, meaning 'The Falcon,' Daud Beg, who later adopted the name of Çagrı Beg, and Ibrahim ibn Inal, found an excuse for again attacking the Ghaznavids in the murder of Yusuf, a grandson of Seljuk, who had been in command of a Turkish unit of the Ghaznavid army. Before setting out on the campaign Tügrül ventured to write to the Caliph to give him his version of the quarrel, to pledge his loyalty and to ask in return for the Caliph's approval of his action. Mikail may have been killed in the fighting which followed, for in 1030 only his sons were in command of the army. They managed to inflict severe losses on their enemy and the peace which was agreed upon in 1034 gave the Seljuks control over the whole of Horasan. Tügrül and Daud proclaimed themselves the sup/ porters of the Abbasid Caliphs and, in the following year, both were invested with the governorship of Dihistan, Naza and Farawa, both receiving the double/peaked caps, rich robes and great standards which, according to Persian custom, consti/ tuted their badges of office, as well as the gift of caparisoned horses and gold belts, together with thirty pieces of cloth, prescribed by Turkish custom.[10]

MIKAIL

It was at about this time that Israil's son reappeared in Buhara, having escaped from Ghazna after seven years of captivity. His return and the news of Israil's death served as an excuse for yet

TÜGRÜL

another Seljukid attack on Ghazna. Once again Tügrül and his brothers commanded their armies, whilst the Ghaznavids were led by Mahmud's heir, Mesud. In 1040 their quarrel was finally settled in the battle fought at Dandarqan, near Merv, when victory again fell to the Seljuks. This time it was con-clusive and the Ghaznavids were forced to abandon all their western territory, and to withdraw behind the walls of Ghazna. The Seljuks were left secure in Horasan, whilst in Ghazna, with his spirit broken by his defeat, Mesud laid aside his sword and immersed himself in music and wine. Bands of fierce Turcomans took advantage of the Ghaznavid collapse to move westward and to begin their gradual but sustained infiltration into the eastern provinces of Byzantium, where they proceeded to roam at will, terrifying the settled population of the area.

The victory of Dandarqan was the first in a long series of triumphs which was ultimately to carry the Seljuks right across Persia and Iraq into Syria and Asia Minor. Tügrül realized that it had placed the whole of Persia within his grasp. By 1043 he had consolidated his hold on Tabaristan and moved his capital to Merv. He then penetrated into India, establishing his headquarters at Nishapur, to proclaim himself the Protector of the Abbasid Caliph; in return, that prelate recognized Tügrül's assumption of sovereign powers by reading his name in the Kutba or official prayer recited in the Great Mosque at Baghdad on Fridays and on state occasions, giving it prece-dence over that of the city's Buyid suzerain, al Malık.

Tügrül considered that the time had now come for him and his brothers to separate, and whilst Çagrı set out to conquer the Muslim lands lying to the east of the Tigris, Tügrül sent Ibrahim against Hamadan and the Jebel. Both prospered, but Ibrahim more so than Çagrı, for he managed to establish him-self so securely in the north-western area of Persia that in 1045 he was able, with the help of Ghuzz reinforcements, to press forward into Armenian territory. His advance took the form of a quick succession of brilliantly conducted raids directed against Manzikert, Erzurum and Trebizond, but the spectacular nature of these achievements roused the jealousy which is never dormant for long in a nomad's envious and suspicious mind. Inevitably, Tügrül began to doubt his brother's loyalty and Ibrahim became aware of these misgivings. Fearing for his life he found it expedient to cede Hamadan to his elder brother and suzerain lord, but the transaction left him angry and resentful. Henceforth hatred smouldered bitterly within Ibrahim.

As ruler of the whole of north-eastern Persia and much of Azerbaidzhan, Tügrül decided once again to move his capital, setting it up this time in the delightful town of Rey, where his favourite nephew Alp Arslan, the Lion, a son of his beloved brother Çagrı, remained with him. In accordance with the old Ghuzz custom he established certain of his male relatives as local governors, investing them with the powers of semi-independent vassals, and since he himself remained acutely conscious of his responsibilities as the Caliph's champion, he never allowed them to forget this duty to their spiritual chief. Thus, when the weak and ineffectual Caliph al Qu'aim permitted himself to become the pawn of the Turk Başasırı, the representative of al Malık, the last Buyid ruler of Fars, Tügrül felt obliged to intervene. In 1055 he set out at the head of his army for Baghdad, determined to secure the Caliph's independence. Once again fortune favoured him; Baghdad quickly capitulated, and although Tügrül took advantage of his success to assume the temporal powers which had been vested in the Abbasids, but which the Buyids had seized from them, he did nevertheless faithfully restore to the Caliph much of his former prestige by reinvesting him with the powers of supreme spiritual ruler of Islam, allowing him to retain in that capacity the services of a vizir.[11] In return, in the year 1058, the Caliph heaped imperial honours on his valiant protector, placing a sumptuous robe on Tügrül's shoulders, seating him on a

Fig. 1

magnificent throne and proclaiming him Sovereign of the East and West. This cordiality was reinforced soon after by the Caliph's marriage to Tügrül's niece, Arslan Hatun Khadiça, a sister of Alp Arslan. The ceremony was celebrated in Baghdad with great splendour. In 1063, when aged about seventy, Tügrül died in Rey of a haemorrhage, on the eve of his own marriage to the Caliph's daughter.

ALP
ARSLAN
1063–1072

Alp Arslan had served Tügrül loyally and he might well have been ready to do likewise for his brother Süleyman, the rightful heir, had not Kutulmuş, a son of Israil, set out to contest the crown. Alp Arslan took up arms against the claimant. Their troops met in battle at Damgan. In the course of the fighting Kutulmuş fell from his horse and, in doing so, fractured his skull and died on the spot. Alp Arslan lost no time in assuming the crown. He was to prove worthy of his throne. Both his appearance and his character fitted him for the role of sovereign; he was extremely tall, yet he added to the impression created by his great height by wearing an immensely high hat, and he grew his moustache so long that, when out hunting, he was obliged to knot its ends behind his head that they should not interfere with his aim. His strength was as great as his aim was true, yet his valour exceeded both. Indeed, he was as noble and brave in his conduct as he was magnificent in appearance. Austere in his way of life, unspoilt in his taste and sincere in his behaviour, he was by nature extremely chivalrous. He generally treated his enemies with courtesy; he was generous, often distributing large sums of money among the poor and showing himself ready to relieve distress by money gifts or grant of pensions. On the other hand he did not always succeed in mastering his hot temper, and when his feelings were deeply involved could act as harshly as his uncle Tügrül.

Alp Arslan was also an excellent judge of men, and chose his advisers wisely. He had a natural respect for learning, and

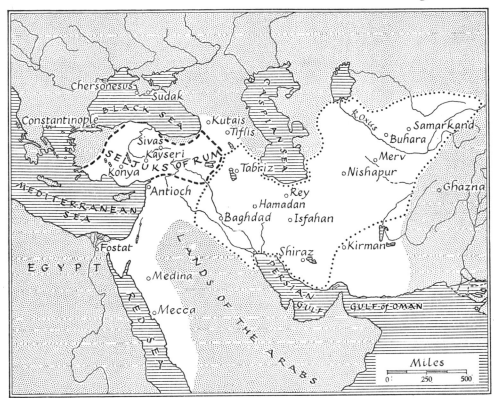

Fig. 1. Map showing the territories ruled by the Seljuks, but with special reference to those of the Great Seljuks of Persia.

this was fostered in him by his remarkable vizir, the Nizam al Mulk. Under the latter's guidance Alp Arslan came to delight in the company of scholars and artists, but his greatest pleasure lay in listening to the tales of chivalry of the heroes of Persia's past. These provided him with inspiration for his own conduct, spurring him to perform acts of daring which were in their turn immortalized by the poets gathered at his court. With their aid no less than by virtue of his own personality, his achievements

C

as a ruler, a military commander and a patron of the arts set a standard which subsequent Seljukid rulers strove to equal. Not all of them were able to achieve such a success in all three capacities, but Alaeddin Keykûbad I of Rum came the closest to doing so.

Alp Arslan established his reputation as a military commander by capturing Herat within a year of assuming power. In the course of another twelve months he had conquered Djand, where his great-grandfather Seljuk had been buried, had restored order in the unsettled districts of Fars and Kirman, retaken the holy cities of Mecca and Medina from the Fatimids, and captured Aleppo. The marriage of his son Malık to a Ghaznavid princess helped to pacify his eastern and southern boundaries. Thus, though his kingdom stretched from the frontiers of Afghanistan to those of Fatimid Egypt, only his western boundaries remained unsecured. These now abutted in the south-east on to the military zone which the Byzantines had been obliged to establish on a line running from Antioch to Malatya in order to prevent the Arabs from infiltrating into the Empire.

Muslim encroachments in that area had begun to assume dangerous proportions when Tügrül's military reforms, introduced with a view to controlling the Turcomans, led these turbulent nomads to flee the Seljukid empire in ever-increasing numbers and to seek new pasture-lands in eastern Byzantium. It was as much to prevent any further infiltration of the nomads as to safeguard himself from the Seljuks that the Emperor Basil II (976–1025) wished to gain control over Armenia, to turn it into a defence zone of Byzantium similar to that which already existed to the south-east.

Yet despite the measures taken in the south-eastern zone, the Islamic element within the Byzantine border continued to be strengthened by the constant influx into the protected area of militant Muslims and marauding Turks, whose joint activities made it ever more difficult for the Greeks to maintain communications, to safeguard the towns in that area and to keep the rural population reasonably prosperous and contented. Some of the Muslims even managed to establish themselves in certain districts as wellnigh autocratic princelings, and it was this as much as anything which finally made the Emperor decide, in about the year 1000, to try to persuade the Georgian and Armenian sovereigns to cede their territories to him. The Georgian Curopolate David eventually agreed to hand over Iberia[12] and, in 1020, the Emperor ventured to approach the King of Armenia with a similar request. Negotiations between them dragged on for two years, but eventually the King became convinced of the seriousness of the Seljukid threat and agreed to relinquish his kingdom in exchange for a new fief situated in the Taurus, which was to have Sebaste (Sivas) as its capital.[13]

The Emperor would perhaps have been wiser had he allowed Armenia to remain responsible for its own security, for the Greek military machine was in such a parlous state, as a result of the stringent economy measures taken by his predecessor, that he was in no position to safeguard Byzantium's existing frontiers, let alone any addition to them. Tügrül discovered Byzantium's weak spot in 1045 when a Seljukid assault penetrated to the shores of Lake Van and to Kars. In 1047 the Byzantines were only just able to hold a second Seljukid attack, aimed this time at Erzurum. In the following year the Seljuks renewed their offensive, breaching that town's defences and plundering the inhabitants. In 1049 they pillaged Ani; in 1053 they once again attacked Kars; in 1056 they sacked Melitene, and in 1059 they even made a rapid incursion into Sebaste.

Although these assaults took the form of raids rather than of planned campaigns, they were nevertheless highly organized and soldierly affairs. The men concerned in them were sent to a prearranged meeting-point where they were divided into four groups of equal strength and drawn up in a square formation to face the four points of the compass. Then each section advanced to another predetermined point, where each again divided, this time into three units of equal size, when the entire force swept forward simultaneously, spreading out in a fan-like formation to loot and destroy everything in its path till the target had been reached. Finally, all rapidly withdrew with their booty, reassembling in accordance with the method they had used for their advance.

Though Alp Arslan was primarily concerned with the conquest of Herat, he in his turn crossed the Araxes in 1064 in order to attack Ani, the capital of the last independent emir of Kars, in the hope of thereby deterring the Byzantines from concluding an alliance with his arch-enemies the Fatimids. After inflicting heavy damage on the town the Seljuks swung south to pillage Antioch and Edessa (Urfa), but in the following year Alp Arslan resumed his incursions into Asia Minor. In 1067 he stormed Caesaraea (Kayseri), defeating the Byzantine armies at Levitane and Sebaste. Thus encouraged, in 1068 he determined to force an entry into Byzantium proper. Accordingly, in the following year, he broke through to the walls of Iconium (Konya) and in another twelve months he had attacked Chonas on the Aegean.

In Byzantium the throne was occupied at the time by Constantine Ducas (1059–67), a liberal-minded emperor, whose intellectual tastes and democratic opinions were shared and encouraged by his former tutor Michael Psellos, who now held the post of chief minister. Together they made many errors in administration, but their greatest mistake consisted in the drastic cuts which they imposed on the budgets of the fighting services. These led to a reduction in the salaries of the officer classes and a decrease in the number of paid reservists, and so to general inefficiency. Not only the army suffered; the canker

spread to those in charge of the arsenals and stores, and even
the frontier garrisons became dangerously depleted. Soon many
districts in the eastern provinces became depopulated, and the
Turcoman nomads and petty Turkish chieftains in these areas
were found to outnumber the native Greeks.

When Constantine died the Empire was scarcely in a position to defend itself, and his son and heir, Michael VII, was
still too young to assume control. At this critical juncture the
boy's mother, the Empress Eudoxia, came forward to act as
regent, but a powerful group opposed her on the ground that
the situation required a stronger hand than hers. To settle the
matter Eudoxia decided to marry again. She chose as her
second husband Romanos IV Diogenes (1067-71), a pro-
fessional soldier and a commander of distinction.

The new Emperor was very much alive to the difficulties
confronting him, for he realized that although the Seljuks were
still content to do little more than raid and plunder Byzantine
territory, the situation could only deteriorate if it were allowed
to drift on. Like Basil II, he thought it essential to control
Armenia so as to transform it into a bulwark of Byzantium,
and he therefore determined to try to evict the Seljuks from
that country. With this end in view he set about assembling
an army, but to succeed he was forced to employ mercenaries
of various nationalities. He enrolled Norsemen, Franks, Slavs,
Turks of diverse origins—such as Cumans, Ghuzz or even
Turks from southern Russia, as well as Petchenegs, many
of whom broke away at the first opportunity. He was also
obliged to rely on Sicilians as officers and even on an occasional
Crusader. Romanos decided to command this motley force in
person, for he was well aware of the poor quality of many of
his regiments. He chose a time when Alp Arslan was busy
campaigning in Egypt to lead 200,000 men eastward, hoping
to be able to take Armenia by surprise. And, indeed, the
opening, mainly defensive phase of the campaign, embracing

the summer months of 1069, was not without success. Thus emboldened the Emperor decided to launch his major attack in 1070/71.

When his forces had drawn near to the Armenian border Romanos divided them into two groups, sending one to capture Ahlat, while he led the other towards Manzikert (also known as Malazgirt). When news of his movements was reported to Alp Arslan, the Sultan entrusted the conduct of his affairs in Egypt to his vassal Atzis ibn Abaq, who was to take advantage of his new powers to capture Jerusalem in 1071. Turning his back on Egypt Alp Arslan hurried northward at the head of a strong army, determined on giving battle to Romanos. Luck favoured him, for the Emperor was not informed of this new development till the Seljukid army was close at hand, when it was too late for him to reunite his force with the one which had been sent to occupy Ahlat. Yet Romanos was so obsessed by the idea of catching up with the rest of his army that he pressed forward without sending scouts to reconnoitre along his line of advance. The Greeks were to pay dearly for the shortcomings of their intelligence service and for their Emperor's carelessness.

BATTLE OF MANZIKERT On the fateful morning of Friday, 19th August 1071, by feigning a withdrawal Alp Arslan contrived to trap the bulk of the vast Byzantine army in a valley on the outskirts of Manzikert. During the night the Petcheneg, Ghuzz and Cuman mercenaries—all of them men of Turkish origin and some of them kinsmen of the Seljuks—deserted from the Byzantines.[14] In the morning, even though his forces had become seriously depleted, Romanos could not avoid giving battle; his men still outnumbered those of Alp Arslan, who are thought not to have exceeded 150,000, and even now all might have gone well for the Greeks had not the Emperor's Frankish troops chosen this moment to refuse to take part in the contest. The fighting which ensued, while they watched it from afar, was bitter in the extreme, but the Byzantines proved no match for the Seljuks, and the Greeks fled in panic before the fierceness of the onslaught. Breaking up into small bands they forgot, in their fear and confusion, to safeguard the person of their sovereign. Abandoned even by his bodyguard, the Emperor was captured by Alp Arslan's men.

The Greeks had suffered a shattering defeat, the consequences of which were to prove disastrous to them. From the start both combatants realized the significance of the event that had taken place, and although in due course the Emperor obtained his release by the payment of a ransom of one and a half million dinars, thereafter, when speaking of the battle, the Byzantines never referred to it otherwise than as 'that dreadful day'. The peace terms were agreed upon by Romanos while he was still a prisoner; they were extremely harsh, for in addition to the heavy ransom which he had had to pay to secure his freedom, he had to agree to a fifty-year truce and to the release of all the Muslim prisoners held by the Byzantines. Most ignominious of all, he had to undertake to provide the Selujkid army with a contingent of Byzantine troops whenever these should be demanded.

While Romanos was agreeing to these terms in Armenia, Michael had had himself proclaimed emperor in Constantinople. The new monarch was a weak creature and quite unfit for the task on hand. When Romanos returned to the capital civil war broke out between the supporters of each sovereign. Eventually the monarchs themselves entered into secret negotiations and, having been assured of his personal safety, Romanos voluntarily surrendered—only to find that the promised immunity, though guaranteed by the highest dignitaries of the State, was not to be granted. At Michael's orders he was cruelly blinded and imprisoned in a monastery on one of the Princes' Islands, where, broken hearted, he died of his wounds within the year.

Romanos had not misjudged the extent of the danger threatening Byzantium from the east, for Alp Arslan also realized that the victory of Manzikert had opened the road for Seljukid penetration westward. Indeed, he felt so confident of the final outcome that he decided to abide by the terms of the treaty and defer further operations in this sector to a future date. Instead he turned his attention to Turkestan. The ostensible reason for the expedition which he led into Central Asia in 1072 was to restrain the Shah of Kwarazm, whose growing power gave cause for concern. The future was to justify these fears, for on the death of Alp Arslan's son Malık Shah, the Kwarazmian rulers were to usurp many of the powers of the Great Seljuks, and eventually, at the dynasty's collapse following upon the death of Sultan Sencer in 1157, to form an empire which comprised much of northern Persia in addition to their own Central Asian territories.

Meanwhile the campaign was to prove Alp Arslan's last. Death came to him in a strange manner, befalling him as he sat in judgement over a band of captives which included a Kwarazmian commander called Yusuf. The latter was brought before the Sultan pinioned, and when Alp Arslan pronounced the death sentence upon him the bound man hurled abuse at the conqueror. Stung to the quick by his taunts, Alp Arslan ordered the guards to loosen Yusuf's bonds and to stand aside; then the Sultan raised his bow and shot an arrow at his captive; but fate chose this moment to play a cruel trick on the best marksman of his day, for the king's arrow went wide of the man and in the moment of consternation which followed Yusuf sprang at Alp Arslan, killing him with a blow from his dagger.

With the death of Alp Arslan the story of the Great Seljuks of Persia, the name by which the dynasty was distinguished from the other Seljukid kingdoms, ceases to have any very direct bearing on that of the Seljuks of Rum, for although two of his successors, Malık Shah and Bargıyaruk, as suzerains over the younger branch of the family, made their influence felt once or twice, their role was never an all-important one. The time was now approaching for the Seljuks of Rum to play their part in shaping the course of events in Asia Minor, and for the Great Seljuks to recede from the scene, and soon entirely to disappear from it.

CHAPTER II

The History of the Seljuks of Rum

IT WAS THE CUSTOM of the Great Seljuks—one which they had acquired from their nomadic ancestors—to establish their closest male relations as minor princelings or governors over their more distant territories. Each of these deputies was allowed considerable independence as long as he recognized the Sultan as his sovereign and accepted the latter's decisions on all aspects of foreign policy. It was in accordance with this principle that the Great Seljukid rulers also allowed certain vanquished kings to retain their thrones provided that they accepted the ties of vassalship. These concessions were gradually extended to include commanders who had distinguished themselves in battle; later the Nizam al Mulk was to advocate the revival of the system of monetary rewards for gallantry in the field, and when he failed to carry this suggestion, he was at pains to stress that the gift of a fief did not entitle the holder to regard the local people as his serfs or permit him to levy more than a limited sum of money from them. The system as a whole was designed to keep potential claimants to the throne too busy dealing with administrative matters to plot for supreme power, but it had certain disadvantages. Nomadic chieftains are particularly prone to jealousy and intrigue; the powers inherent in the office of governor helped to foster these tendencies, whilst the sense of responsibility which is sometimes derived from kingship was no longer present to keep ambition in check. Thus frequent outbreaks of disloyalty continued to occur among the very princes who should have been satisfied in ruling over the provinces which their suzerain had entrusted to their care. The sultans were therefore obliged to be constantly on the alert, always holding themselves ready to march from one far-flung corner of their vast empire to the other so as to maintain order. In consequence the powers of the Great Seljukid rulers tended to grow weaker as the size of their empire increased, and the minor princes of the house and the local emirs, many of whom were of Turkish origin, in contrast to the civil servants who were generally either Persians or Arabs, were quick to take advantage of any sign of laxity in order to pay no more than lip service to their monarchs. Gradually, therefore, outlying portions of the empire broke loose from the mother state.

Alp Arslan's victory at Manzikert had opened the road to Seljukid penetration into Asia Minor, but when the Sultan decided to march against the Shah of Kwarazm instead of exploiting his advantage, the choice of the commander to be left in charge of affairs on the western front became a matter of considerable importance. It is impossible to determine the means by which Süleyman, a young prince of the royal house, obtained the office, for although a first-cousin-once-removed of Alp Arslan, he was the son of Kutulmuş, the very man who, though loyal to Tügrül, had contested the throne left vacant at that sovereign's death and had died at Rey fighting to obtain it. Nevertheless, it was Süleyman who, on Alp Arslan's departure, took charge of affairs in the north-western zone. The office was no sinecure; it demanded considerable abilities from the holder, for the Seljuks were of the opinion that the death of the Emperor Romanos invalidated the peace treaty which had been concluded after the battle of Manzikert. It was part of Süleyman's task to administer the conquered territory in such a manner as to make it abundantly clear to the Turkish chieftains and to the nomad Turcomans who had penetrated into the region that the Seljuks were their masters, while at the same time making preparations for the eventual resumption of hostilities against the Byzantines.

SÜLEYMAN 1077–1086

In Constantinople, the bookish and pacifist Emperor Michael was appalled by the danger threatening Byzantium on its eastern boundary. In his anxiety he sent impassioned appeals for help to Pope Gregory VII. The Pope in his turn, though with somewhat diminished anguish, invoked Christen‐dom to come to the aid of the Eastern Church. Meanwhile Michael, distracted by the dilatoriness with which the Western world was responding to his entreaties, endeavoured to muster an army by hastily enrolling any mercenaries who came his way. Among the officers whom he engaged in this manner was the Norman, Roussel of Bailleul, perhaps the most covetous and least dependable of all the barons who flocked to Con‐stantinople in the hope of gaining for themselves the best of both worlds, securing some of the wealth of the Levant while seek‐ing, by their crusading activities, to ensure the salvation of their souls.

Roussel set out to gain Michael's confidence and then, at a crucial moment, the perfidious Norman abandoned the Greek army to its fate and, in flagrant disregard of his oath of allegi‐ance, set out to try to carve a fief for himself in Anatolia. But this did not represent the full extent of his villainy for, doubting his ability to succeed in this disloyal scheme, he did not hesitate to appeal to Süleyman, the Greek Emperor's most dangerous enemy, to come to his aid. Appreciating the advantages to be drawn from such an alliance Süleyman readily agreed to join forces with the Christian rebel, and together the leaders had little difficulty in defeating the imperial army at Armorium (some 34 miles to the west of present‐day Sıvrıhisar). Its com‐mander, Caesar John Ducas, was captured and crowned Emperor by the Norman at Nicomedia (Izmit).

The crowning of John Ducas was followed by disturbances throughout Byzantium which persisted for the best part of twenty years, assuming at times the character almost of civil war. Malık Shah, who had succeeded to the throne of the Great Seljuks, watched these developments with attention, noting Süleyman's skill in the diplomatic sphere no less than in the military till, in about 1077/78, he felt justified in appoint, ing him Governor of Rum. This promotion may well have helped to decide Michael, who was still suffering from the shock caused by the treachery of his Norman ally, to follow the dangerous precedent Roussel had set by appealing in his turn to Süleyman for help against the insurgents. Before sending a reply Süleyman consulted Malık Shah, his suzerain lord; the Sultan did not delay in acquiescing, for he too was well aware of the benefits that might be derived from the arrangement.

Süleyman was therefore able to enter Byzantium proper as its sovereign's welcome ally, riding into the coveted land at the head of a considerable army. Luck favoured the Seljuk, for he soon succeeded in capturing Roussel, whom he then dis, honestly refused to deliver to the Emperor until the latter had paid over a considerable ransom for the Norman. Having done so, the Byzantines kept Roussel a prisoner for only a short time, for the simultaneous appearance in 1078 of two further claimants for the imperial throne forced the Emperor to rally all available help round his person. Roussel was released on promising to defend the legitimate sovereign.

The two claimants who had come forward almost at the same moment appeared in different parts of the empire. The one, Nicephorus Botaniates advanced from the west, proclaim, ing himself Emperor on reaching Adrianople and then con, tinuing his march on Constantinople. The other rebel, Nice, phorus Briennius, had been active in Asia Minor where he had been enrolling the Greek refugees from Manzikert into his army, but his cause met with only lukewarm support and his force remained so small that he too decided in his turn to apply to Süleyman for help! The Seljuk was only too glad to add to the general confusion by coming to the assistance of yet another Christian. Thus it was that the combined regiments of the insurgent Greeks and the invading Seljuks advanced west, ward together, capturing first Cysicus and then Nicaea, where the pretender was proclaimed Emperor. Then, still proceeding side by side, both armies entered Nicomedia, whence they marched on Chalcedone, to push on the Chrysopolis (the modern Kadikoy), a town lying on the Asiatic shore of the Marmara. There they separated; and while the Greek commander crossed the waters to Constantinople, to depose the Emperor and assume full powers, the Seljuk entrenched himself on the Asiatic shore to gaze across the sparkling sea to the heart of Christendom, the very epitome of imperial power.

Nicephorus Briennius's assumption of power in 1078 set off a new revolt among the Greeks of Asia Minor. The rising was led by a General, Nicephorus Melissenus, who, following what had now become virtually a routine among the Christian insurgents of the area, in his turn appealed to Süleyman for aid. Once again the Seljuks proved ready to oblige, and once again a Christian and a Muslim force advanced into Bithynia side by side. There the Byzantine garrisons, which were largely formed of Turkish mercenaries, deserted to the Seljuks whom they regarded as kinsmen. As a result Melissenus found his force so heavily depleted that he was obliged to abandon the idea of advancing on Constantinople. Instead he decided to entrench himself in Bithynia and he requested his ally to withdraw from the area. This time, however, Süleyman did not fall in with the Greek's suggestion, nor was the General in any position to enforce his request, so that Süleyman was able to take advantage of the situation to annex Lydia and Ionia, and to establish there the first Seljukid emirate to be formed on Anatolian soil. In 1078 he proclaimed Nicaea his capital and declared himself Sultan.

NICAEA AS CAPITAL Süleyman was now able to pause and take stock of the situation. It was indeed an enviable one, for although a host of Turkish princelings had followed in his rear, some of them establishing themselves as autonomous rulers over considerable

Fig. 2. Map of the Seljukid Empire, but with special reference to that of the Seljuks of Rum.

areas, the Seljuks had nevertheless taken possession of a very large tract of land in which they controlled many towns of importance. Indeed, the conquered area formed a veritable kingdom, for it comprised much of Armenia and stretched across most of Asia Minor almost to the Hellespont, including to the south-east many districts which had formerly belonged to the Emir of Aleppo. In the west a strip of land on the outskirts of Smyrna (Izmir) formed a valuable fief belonging to the power-ful Turkish Emir Tzakas; it served as a sort of no-man's-land which both the Greeks and the Seljuks avoided, the Greeks through weakness, the Seljuks because, in contrast to Tzakas himself, they failed to appreciate the advantages that were to be derived from the control of a maritime port.

Süleyman's lack of interest in this western region and his

Fig. 2

failure to appreciate the value of an outlet to the sea was caused in part by his preoccupation with Syria and Egypt, where the religion and native Islamic culture were familiar and dear to him, riveting his interest and ambitions. Notwithstanding the spectacular nature of his victories he could never seriously have envisaged himself challenging and succeeding to the might of Byzantium; and his choice of Nicaea as a capital was probably due rather to the city's geographical advantages than to any strong desire to humiliate the Greek Emperor, for the town's position astride the road connecting Constantinople to Jeru-salem made it a convenient centre from which to control both Asia Minor and Syria.

When Süleyman proclaimed Nicaea his capital something very like panic broke out among the inhabitants of Asia Minor. Nomad Turcoman refugees mingled with the terrified Christians who sought refuge beyond the reach of Seljukid power, many of the Armenians fleeing to the Armenian fiefs in the Taurus and anti-Taurus known to them as 'Little Ar-menia'. The deep impression which this event made in Chris-tendom as a whole can to some extent be gauged from the numerous references to Süleyman which occur in the tales of chivalry which were so popular at the time in Western Europe.

In Constantinople a new Emperor, Alexios, had come to the throne in 1081. In Asia he was faced with a situation which he could not hope to control till he had restored order in his capital and in his western provinces. Though the task took five years to complete he was able as early as 1083 to turn his atten-tion eastward. Determining to regain his Asiatic lands, he crossed the Marmara and marched against Süleyman. The Seljuk withdrew, following nomadic practice by setting fire to the crops as he did so. Fearing a famine if he pushed too far forward Alexios hesitated between attacking Iconium (Konya) or Philomelium (Akşehir). His daughter relates that he settled the question by writing the name of each town on a piece of paper, after which he spent the night in prayer; then, at dawn, 'in the presence of all' a priest picked up one of the folded pieces, of paper and read out the name of Philomelium. The Emperor thereupon marched upon the city and forced the enemy to give battle. The fighting was long drawn out. In the course of it the Emperor's son, Andronicos Porphyrogenitos, was killed, but Süleyman was unable to prevent the Byzantines from retaking Nicomedia, and in the peace negotiations which followed Süleyman had to agree to a form of vassalship. But on his side the Emperor had to abandon certain territories to the Seljuks, though to save his face he pretended that he had ceded them to Süleyman on a colonization grant.[15]

With the *status quo* thus established Süleyman's thoughts turned eastward again. In 1086, leaving his wife and children at Nicaea, he set out for Antioch, hoping to capture it in a rapid assault, but the city's defences proved impregnable and he was obliged to strike camp outside the town. The governor of Antioch was an Armenian called Philaretos. During the siege either he or his son turned traitor and helped the Seljuks to enter secretly and capture the town. The fall of Antioch enabled Süleyman to declare himself independent of the Great Seljuks, an announcement which aroused the fears of the Muhammadan princes of Syria who now found themselves his neighbours. Forming themselves into a coalition they sent Süleyman a joint challenge. The Seljuk replied to the threat by advancing on Aleppo. The city's governor panicked and appealed to Tutuş of Syria, the brother of the Great Seljukid sultan Malık Shah, for aid. As Tutuş's jealousy had also been aroused he gladly hastened to the relief of the threatened city. The enemies met in battle in 1086, almost midway between Aleppo and Antioch.

The fighting was severe and prolonged, but the outcome remained indefinite until, according once again to Anna Comnena,[16] it developed into a hand-to-hand conflict, when Süleyman's men suddenly broke their ranks and fled. Finding

D

himself unable to stem the panic the Sultan turned to escape; then, in the words of the Greek princess,[17] 'when he thought he had reached a safe spot he put his shield on the ground and sat on it. He was followed by an observer, who said that Tutuş wished to see him. Thereupon Süleyman quickly drew his sword from its sheath and plunged it deep into his bowels; and thus the wretched man died wretchedly.'

The unexpectedness of Süleyman's death and the magnitude of his defeat upset the stability of Anatolia, and quarrels at once broke out between the various Turkish princelings who now claimed the empty throne. Malık Shah, ruler of the Great Seljuks, availed himself of the unrest to intervene, for he too had watched Süleyman's spectacular rise to power with considerable concern. Resuming responsibility for Asia Minor he appointed two generals governors of Rum and took Süleyman's second son back to Isfahan with him as a hostage in place of the elder, who was already held captive in Iraq. On Malık Shah's death in 1092 Bargıyaruk ascended the throne. The new ruler was a weaker and a kinder man than his father, and one of his first acts as sovereign was to release Süleyman's son, who was thus able in the course of the same year to proclaim himself Sultan of the Seljuks of Rum under the title of Kılıçarslan I.

KILIÇAR-
SLAN I
1092–1107

On his return to Nicaea Kılıçarslan found it difficult to regain control of affairs, for at Süleyman's death a Turkish rebel named Abu 'l Kasim had installed himself in the capital and reduced the kingdom to a state of chaos. The Byzantine Emperor had been quick to add to the instability by all methods open to him short of warfare, and by 1096 it seemed as though his propaganda campaign would of itself succeed in ending Seljukid rule in Asia Minor. Indeed, the situation seemed so favourable to the Greeks that the Crusaders induced the Emperor to join them in an attempt to expel the Muslims from Asia Minor with a view to reopening the pilgrim road to the Holy Land. In accordance with this plan units of the First Crusade set out under the leadership of Walter the Penniless to evict the Seljuks from Nicaea; but the force was ill-disciplined and poorly led, so that even though Kılıçarslan had not had time properly to prepare for the battle he had little difficulty in winning it. The ease with which he did so was to prove unfortunate for him in the long run, for it led him greatly to underestimate the fighting qualities of the Christian armies.

Had Kılıçarslan not underrated the seriousness of the Chris- THE
tian threat, it is hardly likely that he would have chosen this DANIŞMEND
moment to abandon his capital in order to march eastward to fight the Danişmend of the Sivas-Kayseri area who, at the instigation of the Byzantines, had begun to advance against Malatya (Melitene). Like the Seljuks the Danişmend were of Turkish origin. The first of the line, Tailu, had probably known enough written Persian and Arabic to enable him to become a teacher, and his choice of this profession doubtless accounted for that of his dynasty's cognomen. In the twenty years which had elapsed since their first appearance in Anatolia in the wake of the Seljuks, the Danişmend had established themselves as emirs of a district which ultimately came to include Tokat, Niksar, Elbistan and Malatya, and to extend in the north-west to Kastamonu, once the cradle of the Byzan- tine house of Comnene. By the end of the century, under their chieftain Gümüştekin Melik Gazi, they reached the height of their prosperity and even penetrated into Cilicia. The Great Seljuks marked this achievement by conferring on Gümüştekin the black standard, the emblem of authority with which the Abbasids had invested the chieftains who became their autono- mous vassals. The honour entitled the Danişmend to take precedence over Kılıçarslan—a distinction which the latter was determined to ignore and also to avenge.

Kılıçarslan marched eastward against the Danişmend un-
troubled by forebodings, leaving his household and vast
accumulation of treasure seemingly secure at Nicaea. But no
sooner had he departed than a Crusading army led by Raymond of Antioch, the son of Robert Guiscard, together with
Godfrey of Bouillon, Duke of Lorraine, Bohemond and Tancred, advanced upon the city. On 6th May 1097 the Christians
reached Nicaea, but the four miles of great walls, reinforced by
two hundred and fifty massive towers presented a formidable
obstacle, deterring them from launching an immediate attack.
Instead they struck camp outside the town to await the reinforcements which Robert of Normandy, a son of William the
Conqueror and brother to the King of England, together with
Stephen of Blois, were to bring up. The Emperor of Byzantium
encamped at Pelecanum, close to the shore of the Gulf of
Nicomedia, at the head of a Greek army.

News of the siege reached Kılıçarslan whilst he was still on
the march. Abandoning his campaign he hurried back to
defend his capital.

Kılıçarslan reached Nicaea on 21st May to find it encircled
by the enemy. He lost no time in counter-attacking, but
although his men fought superbly he was unable to relieve
the town, and the situation would have reached a stalemate
had not the Greek Emperor conceived the idea of transport-
ing boats overland from Nicomedia to launch them on the
lake at Nicaea.[18] The Seljuks were obliged to watch this
operation from the surrounding hills, powerless to intervene,
while the enemy poured into the town on its only undefended
side. Nicaea capitulated on 26th June, and Alexios arrived from
Pelecanum to take charge of the town. He showed himself not
unchivalrous, for he allowed the Muslim notables to purchase
their liberty, and he despatched the Sultana, her children and
her household to Constantinople in a manner befitting their
royal rank.

The Sultana was the eldest daughter of the Emir Tzakas who controlled, in addition to Smyrna, much of the Aegean coast and the islands of Lesbos, Chios, Samos and even parts of Rhodes. Alexios determined to follow up the liberation of Nicaea by the eviction of Tzakas and his son from Smyrna. Though he was himself committed to Asia Minor, he instructed his commander-in-chief, John Ducas, to proclaim the news of the freeing of Nicaea and, if necessary, to parade the captured Sultana and her children as proof of the victory. At the same time he was to lead an army across the Dardanelles from Abydos to Atramytrion. Ducas had little difficulty in retaking Smyrna. On entering the town he was so greatly angered by the devastation that had been wrought there that he pursued Tzakas's men to Lapadion (Ulubad), where he avenged himself upon them with the utmost savagery. So great was the death role that the surviving Turks donned black as a sign of mourning and 'by this very dress they moved all to pity and roused them to avenge them.'[19] Having no further need of the captured Sultana, Alexios now restored her and her children to Kılıçarslan, without demanding a ransom for their release.

While the Greeks had been inflicting punishment upon Tzakas, the Crusaders had resumed their march towards Antioch and the Holy Land. They had set out from Nicaea along the old military road spanning the Gök Su (Calycadnus) on its way to Dorylaeum (Eskişehir) where a choice of two roads leading across Asia Minor would be open to them. They travelled in two groups; the smaller of these, led by Bohemond, set out ahead of the remainder of the army which was commanded by Godfrey of Bouillon, Raymond of St Gilles and Hugh of Clermont. Meanwhile Kılıçarslan had hurried eastward to make peace with the Danışmend, and to persuade them to forget their quarrel and join him in resisting the Christian invaders. Ties of kinship may well have helped in compelling the Danışmend to agree, and the change of policy was made the easier for them by Kılıçarslan's wish that they should fight the Crusaders rather than the Byzantines, whom the Danışmend tended to regard as to some extent their protectors. But the Seljuks were not alone in so quickly gaining an ally, for the Crusaders found unexpected support among the Fatimids who, as inveterate enemies of the Seljuks, were assisting the Ortokid rulers of the Mardin-Hisn Kaifa regions to resist Kılıçarslan.

The Ortokids were also Turks of Ghuzz extraction. They owed their rise to power to Tutuş of Damascus who, on capturing Jerusalem in 1086, had appointed the Ortokid Urtuk b Aksab to become the city's governor, as a reward for the gallantry which he had displayed two years earlier when assisting the Sultan of the Great Seljuks to besiege Amida. At his death in 1094 Urtuk was succeeded in office by his sons Sukman and Ilghazi, but in 1104/05 Sukman, the elder of the two, assumed the powers of an independent sovereign, adding Mardin to his territory.

BATTLE OF
DORY-
LAEUM

Having become allies, the Seljuks and the Danışmend lost no time in setting out in pursuit of the Crusaders. Hurrying behind them, they succeeded in catching up with Bohemond's force on a June evening in 1097 as it lay encamped on the outskirts of Dorylaeum. Assuming that the men gathered round the fires represented the entire Christian force, the Muslims attacked at dawn on the following day. The Turks were in the habit of advancing in three independent groups, so that whichever section became involved in the fighting first, the other two could, in the words of Anna Comnena,[20] 'turn like whirlwinds and throw the opposing body into confusion.' The men seldom used spears but relied on their mobility to enable them to surround the enemy and then to hail arrows on him from a distance, sending the archers forward in successive waves.

'When a Turk pursues', the Byzantine princess summed up bitterly, 'he captures his man with a blow; when he is pursued, he conquers with darts; he throws a dart and the flying dart hits the horse or the rider, piercing whichever is hit.'

At the outset fortune favoured the Seljuks at Dorylaeum, but in the afternoon strong Christian reinforcements came up, striking the Muslims in the rear and, towards evening, the Muslims weakened till their men suddenly fled in disorder, abandoning their stores, tents and valuables. This defeat was a major one and it helped to offset some of the advantages which the Seljuks had gained twenty years earlier at the battle of Manzikert; but their soldiers had displayed such bravery in the fighting that even the *Geste Francorum* was later to pay tribute to their valour.

The Christians had also suffered serious losses in the battle, and they decided to pursue their journey to the Holy Land travelling as a single unit. Not realizing its difficulties, they chose the shorter route through Philomelium to Iconium. The crossing of the Sultan Dag presented terrible hardships to the tired men, weighed down as they were with many wounded and an immense booty. Most of the horses and many of the foot soldiers perished on the march, and the Crusaders were obliged to requisition all manner of beasts to serve as pack-animals, using not only goats and dogs for the purpose, but even pigs. Eventually, the remnants of the victorious army reached Iconium and, after a short rest, the survivors were able to continue on their route.

The battle of Dorylaeum marked a turning-point in Seljukid affairs, for the losses sustained by the Turks both in manpower and wealth were so immense that they put an end to whatever imperialist dreams may have been in their minds. It deprived them of the possession of Iconium, Eregli and Caesarea, while the establishment of Baldwin's kingdom at Edessa and Godfrey of Bouillon's in Palestine set a limit to their expansion

eastward. The presence of a Norman contingent on the Mediterranean coastline in its turn excluded them from the south-
western seaboard. If the Seljuks were to survive at all, it was
essential for them to make themselves masters of Anatolia, and
their innate sense of statesmanship enabled them quickly to
understand this. The odds were not entirely weighted against
their success, for their allies, the Danişmend, with Sivas
(Sebaste) as their capital, had become extremely powerful;
and the Seljuks themselves were still in a position to increase
their army rapidly by enrolling recruits from among the Turcoman nomads, who were entering Asia Minor in ever-increasing
numbers. Furthermore, they held one important asset in the
persons of Bohemond and his cousin Richard of Salerno whom
the Muslim force had succeeded in taking prisoner in 1100
when fighting in the hills near Malatya. Though the Crusaders
had hastened to open negotiations for Bohemond's release, he
was still a prisoner in 1101 owing to their unwillingness to pay
the immense ransom demanded.

While negotiations regarding the ransom were still in progress Raymond of St Gilles returned to Constantinople to meet
a new band of Crusaders arriving from Europe under the command of Count Biandrate. Raymond, as the older and more
experienced man, was eventually put in charge of the joint
force, numbering close on a hundred and fifty thousand men;
but instead of marching to the Holy Land the new arrivals
insisted on being led to Niksar, where Bohemond was imprisoned, in order to secure the latter's release. Advancing
together the two commanders found it easy to capture Ancyra
(Ankara) from the Seljuks, to cross the Kızıl Irmak, and to
turn eastward towards Niksar. But from then onwards the
Seljuks went ahead of them, devastating the crops and destroying the stores in the districts through which they were to pass.

In the intense summer heat the suffering of the invaders soon
became acute; fearing to increase it the Christian commanders

abandoned the idea of rescuing Bohemond and decided to turn northward to Kastamonu, whence they planned to return to Byzantium. However, they were soon forced to relinquish this idea as well, for the men were exhausted by the difficulty of the road, the heat, the scarcity of food and water, and above all by the harassing tactics of the Seljukid guerrillas. The Seljuks attacked the Lombard units, massacred the infantry and forced the cavalry to flee. In complete disregard of Raymond's advice the demoralized survivors insisted on turning eastward again towards Amasya, hoping to find security among the Danışmend.

As they approached their goal Conrad and his German units were ambushed and wiped out. Raymond was obliged to muster all survivors to face the full force of the Muslim attack which followed on 5th August. The armies fought staunchly throughout the day. When night fell and the battle had to be broken off the Seljuks seemed to have fared best; at dawn the next day they hastened to resume the fight. Abandoning their customary tactics they rushed to attack at close quarters with drawn swords. Raymond's men were the first to give way, but surrounded by his bodyguard he managed to break free and to escape to Bafra, a small port on the Black Sea close to Sinop, whence he and his men sailed for Byzantium, leaving the Normans to face total annihilation. The few who survived the slaughter made their way painfully to Cilicia, where they joined Baldwin and Tancred who had been warmly welcomed there by the rich Armenians of the district. Meanwhile the Latins reopened their negotiations for Bohemond's release.

This time they agreed to the terms demanded of them and, in 1103, with the aid of the wealthy Armenian community, the huge ransom was paid to the Danışmend and the prisoner was set free. However, this was not the end of the incident, for Melik Gazi Danışmend became so enamoured of the ransom money that he refused to share it with his Seljukid ally. In the course of the bitter quarrel which resulted Melik did not hesitate to call on the Emperor of Byzantium for aid. War between the erstwhile allies seemed inevitable; it was averted by the timely death of Melik in 1105/06. Even so, the Seljuks never forgave the Danışmend their perfidy and their hatred for them persisted until 1175, when they at last succeeded in wiping out the smaller dynasty.

The quarrel over the ransom did not prevent the Seljuks from continuing to fight the Crusaders, and the war went on, victory going sometimes to the one, sometimes to the other. Yet the Seljuks were able to consolidate their positions steadily and strengthen their hold on Asia Minor, and in the early autumn of 1104 they managed to score a major success at Eregli where they completely destroyed the relief forces which William of Nevers and William of Poitiers had brought over from France. Soon after they attacked another extremely large contingent, made up this time of French, German and other westerners who had hurried over from Europe to retrieve the situation, and once again succeeded in wiping it out. These achievements ensured the security of the Seljukid state, enabling its rulers to turn some of their attention to establishing the administrative services which are essential for stable power.

Unlike the average tribal chieftain who, on achieving victory, thinks only of enjoying its fruits, the Seljuks set out to provide their country with a sound economy and elaborate social services. They applied themselves so seriously to the task that within a few years of these victories a period of very real prosperity dawned for the people of Asia Minor. It was to endure till well into the 13th century, when the advent of the Mongols again brought chaos and poverty to the countryside.

Kılıçarslan was however not in a position to do more than set the new measures in motion, for he was obliged to turn his personal attention to rounding off the boundaries of the new state. With this end in view in 1106 he occupied Malatya and Mayyafarıkın, and in 1107 he entered Mosul and insisted on having his name read in the Kutba in place of that of the Great Seljuk. Throughout he also contrived to send help to the Turkish nomads who were fighting the Georgians, but his attention was diverted from this theatre of war by the wily policy of the Ortokid princes, which had enabled them to raise themselves to a position of supreme importance in the south-eastern corner of Asia Minor. Leaving the Georgian King free to reign over his own country, Kılıçarslan thought it wiser to forestall a future act of Ortokid aggression by provoking their ruler Sukman to battle at a time of his own choosing. Accordingly, in the autumn of 1107, the armies of the two Ghuzz commanders met in the vicinity of Mosul. On this occasion Kılıçarslan's luck failed to hold good, and he died in the course of the fighting, drowning as he crossed the river Habura.

Kılıçarslan's death came as welcome news both to the Emperor of Byzantium and to the Sultan of the Great Seljuks, for neither monarch had felt altogether secure while this brilliant commander had been free to rampage in the vicinity of their long and vulnerable borders. Steven Runciman[21] goes as far as to say that his death 'removed a potential danger from Byzantium at a crucial moment . . . and enabled the Seljuk Sultanate of Persia to endure for nearly a century.' Its effect on his own people was the more serious because it coincided with the captivity of his two elder sons. One—Arap—was a prisoner in Persia, the other—Ruknûddin Mesud—at the Danışmend court. His widow Isabella, a sister of Raymond of St Egidier, nevertheless managed, by acting promptly, to establish the youngest son—Tügrül—as ruler of Malatya and the eastern provinces.

In the emergency the late sovereign's brother, Melik, assumed control, reigning from Konya as Melik Shah I. However, by 1116 Mesud, who had meanwhile married a Danışmend princess, succeeded in persuading his father-in-law and gaoler

MELIK
1107–1116

to release him and assist him in regaining his throne. Their joint efforts on his behalf met with success and Mesud was able to take control of a kingdom which stretched from the Sangarius to the Taurus, though his younger brother still held Malatya and his father-in-law, Danışmend Gazi II, ruled from the Halys to the Euphrates. Mesud wisely concentrated his attention on strengthening his hold on the throne and on enlarging his boundaries at the expense of neighbouring Turkish princelings. At first he was able to count on the help of his father-in-law, who began by wishing to see Mesud sole ruler of Asia Minor and who, in consequence, took advantage of the death in 1124 of the Ortokid ruler to seize some of the latter's lands, though he then developed so great a fondness for these that he refused to hand them over to his son-in-law.

But by this time Mesud was absorbed in a quarrel with his brother Arap. The latter had been released by the Great Seljuks in 1125; hurrying back to Anatolia to reclaim his throne he succeeded quite easily in overthrowing Mesud. The deposed ruler sought refuge in Constantinople. He was well received there by the Emperor and diplomatic talks were held; as a result of these Mesud, helped once again by his Danışmend father-in-law, set out to regain his throne. It did not take him long to depose Arap who, in his turn, sought safety in Constantinople where he too was well received by the Emperor. Indeed, he found life so pleasant in the Byzantine capital that he remained in it till his death many years later. Mesud, on the other hand, established himself in Konya which with Çankırı and Ankara had passed back after the death of Danışmend Gazi II into Seljukid hands, to replace Nicaea as the capital of Rum.

Mesud never forgot the kindness which had been shown to him in Constantinople and it was with the Emperor's knowledge, perhaps even with his approval, that in 1147 he engaged Conrad II and his army in battle; the encounter took place close to Dorylaeum, where Mesud's forebears had suffered an over-whelming defeat. This time it was the Christian force which was destroyed. In the following year Mesud inflicted equally severe punishment on the troops of Louis VII of France, and the king and his courtiers were forced to abandon their men in order to escape to Adalya (Antalya) with their lives, sailing thence to safety. The peace treaty which followed added Maraş to Mesud's territory.

Though Mesud spent most of his reign quarrelling and cam-paigning, at his death in 1156 he left his kingdom in a far stronger position than that in which he had found it. It was now secure, fairly prosperous and influential, and its boundaries had been increased in the east both by the absorption of some of the minor principalities or fiefs which had fallen away from the crumbling empire of the Great Seljuks and also by the annexation of certain Danışmend lands after the death of Gazi II.

Mesud was succeeded on the throne by his son Izzeddin Kılıçarslan II, a prince of quite exceptional ability. Even so, his right to reign was contested by his brother Shahanshah, who established himself in Ankara as claimant, winning the sup-port of Yagı Siyan, the Danışmend Emir of Sivas, who was in his turn sponsored by Nüreddin, the powerful Atabeg of Aleppo. Kılıçarslan was nevertheless able to enlist the support of two minor Danışmend princes, the Emirs Dhu'l Nan of Kayseri and Dhu'l Quarnain of Malatya, and although to begin with Shahanshah and his powerful allies quickly succeeded in regaining the Euphratesian provinces, yet, when the two brothers met face to face, it was Kılıçarslan who defeated Shahanshah.

Almost simultaneously, that is to say in 1158, Kılıçarslan the victor found himself seriously threatened on two fronts, for the Byzantine Emperor Manuel had been quick to assess his reso-luteness and in an effort to forestall some future aggression had

KILIÇAR-
SLAN II
1156–1188

embarked on a policy of encirclement. As a result the Sultan found himself obliged to contend in the west against the combined forces of Nüreddin of Aleppo and of the Danışmend who had become the vassals of Byzantium, and in the north-east against Yakub Arslan, another Danışmend emir. Thus beset he lost some ground in the vicinity of Elbistan in the Anti-Taurus and was also forced back by the Byzantines in the Menander valley. He had indeed no alternative but to sue for peace. The terms agreed upon compelled him to restore certain Asiatic territories to the Greeks, whose frontiers he promised thenceforth to respect; in addition he had to undertake to provide the Byzantine army with contingents of trained Seljukid soldiers whenever required.

In 1161/62, at the conclusion of these negotiations, Kılıçarslan set out on a visit to Constantinople. The Emperor expected him to come as a vassal ready to pay homage to his liege lord, but the Seljuk contrived to appear as a royal guest and to transform the proceedings into a state occasion. He spent several months in the Byzantine capital, enjoying the honours which were heaped upon him, eventually putting his signature to the peace treaty. However, when the time came for his departure he was greatly angered to find that his youngest and favourite son was to be retained as a hostage in Constantinople. In Konya he tried to assuage his rage by arranging to marry the daughter of the Saltukid Emir of Erzurum, but on her way to join him his bride was kidnapped by the Danışmend Yakub Arslan, who wanted her for his nephew. The insult could not be overlooked and, in direct violation of the treaty which he had so recently ratified in Constantinople, Kılıçarslan resumed his war against the Danışmend, recapturing Elbistan and Laranda (Karaman) in 1164, and Cappadocia with the cities of Kayseri and Malatya in 1168, while Ankara fell to him a year later. At the death of Yakub Arslan the Danışmend were able, with the help of Nüreddin of Aleppo, to retake Maraş (Markesi) and Sivas, but Kılıçarslan had nevertheless brought them to the verge of collapse, though it was not until 1175 that the Seljuks succeeded in exterminating the dynasty and annexing the principality.

Kılıçarslan's ability to withstand the Byzantines greatly enhanced his reputation throughout Asia Minor, and Nüreddin, Atabeg of Syria, and the Emperor Manuel of Byzantium both came to regard him with considerable dread; even the great Saladin when he became Emperor of Egypt (1175) viewed him with definite misgivings. The Emperor set out to control the Seljuk's growing might by diplomatic measures, requesting a share of the former Danışmend kingdom on the ground that, as protector of the extinct dynasty, he was entitled to it. The Sultan, as might have been foreseen, refused the demand and, in 1176, Manuel hurriedly despatched an army against Konya, thinking that a rapid thrust might perhaps result in a quick and favourable outcome.

When reports on the size of the invading force reached Kılıçarslan the Sultan thought it wise to send an ambassador to the Emperor to sue for peace, but Manuel no longer trusted the man who had defaulted on a treaty. Refusing to negotiate, he divided the army into two, despatching one section under the command of his cousin Andronicos Vatatze to Paphlagonia. The Seljuks engaged this force in battle near Niksar. Both sides were determined to win the contest and all fought with the utmost determination, but as evening drew near the Seljuks began to gain the upper hand, and by nightfall they had secured a complete victory. In the general confusion Vatatze fell into Seljukid hands, and his captors gleefully severed his head to send it to the Sultan as a trophy.

Nor did Manuel's second army fare better; trapped at Myriokephalon, in the pass of the Sultan Dag above Eğridir, it was virtually wiped out. The Emperor himself compared the disaster to that which his forebears had suffered a hundred years

BATTLE OF MYRIOKEPHALON

earlier at Manzikert. The booty which now fell to the Seljuks was so immense that Kılıçarslan sent part of it to the Caliph as a gift, devoting much of the remainder to the embellishment and fortification of Konya.

In 1179, thinking that he had nothing to fear from Saladin, Kılıçarslan determined to capture the fortress of Ra'ban which guarded the Euphrates on the road leading from Aleppo to Samosate; but Saladin promptly sent a nephew to maintain the existing frontier and Kılıçarslan abandoned the idea. However, in the following year, a more serious dispute strained relations between the two rulers. The trouble was of a personal nature, arising from the recent marriage of Kılıçarslan's dearly-loved daughter Seljuka Hatun, also known as Gevher Nesibi Hatun, to Nüreddin Muhammad, son of the Emir of Hisn Kaifa. Within only a few months of the wedding the young husband had left the princess for a dancing girl of great beauty. Outraged at the insult Seljuka Hatun appealed to her father for redress. The old king set out at the head of his army to avenge her and Nüreddin, panic stricken, fled to Saladin's court.

Kılıçarslan refused to lay down his arms till the towns he had given his daughter as her marriage portion were returned to her. Saladin attempted to settle the quarrel, but having failed to do so he decided to terminate his war against the French Crusaders in order to fulfil his duty to his self-invited guest by confronting Kılıçarslan in battle. The Seljuk was disturbed by the turn of events and bluntly told Saladin that it was unseemly of him to make peace with a Christian in order to fight a Muslim. Saladin replied that it ill-befitted him to abandon a guest; whereupon young Nüreddin intervened, promising to give up his dancing girl and return to his wife if peace were restored.

ABDICATION OF KILIÇAR-SLAN II   By about 1086 Kılıçarslan had begun to feel tired and to believe that his time on earth was running out. The idea of abdicating in favour of his sons started to form in his mind, but remained so nebulous that none knew of it, and Saladin and the Emperor Andronicos, a follower of Manuel, began contemplating an alliance with a view to resisting further Seljukid aggression.

Two years later, when the Sultan was making final arrangements for the division of his kingdom, the secret was still so well kept that Frederick I Barbarossa wrote to ask Kılıçarslan for permission peacefully to traverse Seljukid territory on his way to the Holy Land. Kılıçarslan sent a courteous reply to this letter, but by the spring of 1189, when Frederick, who had wintered at Adrianople (Edirne) was ready to lead his men across the Hellespont and enter the Sultanate, the old sovereign had already abdicated. Unaware of this, Frederick and his army were infuriated when, on crossing the Seljukid border, they found themselves unexpectedly involved in skirmishes against the Turks. Their road took them past Myriokephalon, where the battlefield was still littered with the bones of the Christians who had perished there. The sight made a bad impression on the men and their dejection increased daily as Turkish snipers and guerrillas went into action, harrying their rearguards. Worried and angered at what he regarded as an act of Seljukid treachery, Frederick engaged a Turkish prisoner to guide his army across the grim Sultan Dag to Akşehir and Konya. The route was one of immense difficulty and the guide may well have added intentionally to its trials, for the Crusaders sustained extremely serious losses in men and beasts as they made their arduous way along it. Their suffering was aggravated by the refusal of the local Turkish inhabitants to sell them any food or fodder, and their nerves were frayed by the harassing tactics of the Seljukid guerrillas. When they eventually reached Konya they were exhausted, but Frederick did not stop to take possession of the town. He quickly replenished his supplies and commandeered all the horses and beasts of burden which he found there, then withdrew to the belt of market gardens on its fringe to rest his army for two days before crossing into Cilicia.

E

But he was not destined to reach the Holy Land, for only a few days later, when crossing the Gök Su in the vicinity of Silivke, a stumble flung him into the river's swollen waters, where he perished before his horrified followers could rescue him.

Kılıçarslan's abdication did not bring him the calm which he so ardently desired; rather the reverse, for his last years were poisoned by the bitter quarrels which broke out between his sons. Though he had provided for them all, dividing his kingdom into principalities which he apportioned fairly among them, none was satisfied. Broken hearted, the old Sultan even tually sought refuge with his youngest son, who had been freed by the Byzantines some years earlier. As he lay dying in 1192 he heard that the young prince's right to Konya was being contested by his brother Ruknûddin Süleyman of Tokat. On emerging victorious from this conflict Ruknûddin devoted him self to re establishing the unity of the Sultanate, wisely appointing his brother Mügiseddin Tügrül governor of the newly con quered town of Erzurum. Eventually only his brother Mesud stood out against him at Ankara, but in 1204 Ruknûddin at last contrived to wrest the city from him, murdering Mesud in the process, only to die himself four days later.

KILIÇAR SLAN III 1204

At Ruknûddin's death his emirs elected his son Izzeddin Kılıçarslan III to succeed him, even though the boy was only three years old. Although his uncle's quarrels had prevented the Seljuks from drawing any advantages from the Latin con quest of Constantinople, the throne to which the child ascended was not devoid of lustre, as shortly before his death, Ruknûddin had resumed the war against Georgia and had penetrated into Abkhazia. During Ruknûddin's reign his deposed youngest brother, Giyaseddin Keyhüsrev I, had been living in exile in Constantinople. He had made many friends in the Byzantine capital and had fallen in love with and married a Greek girl of noble birth, a daughter of Manuel Mavrozomos. On seeing his young nephew ascend the throne Giyaseddin began to long for the crown which he believed should have been his by right. His father-in-law encouraged him in his desire to regain it, and within a year he succeeded in doing so. He remained Sultan till his death in 1210.

Keyhüsrev's return to power coincided with the Latin con-quest of Constantinople and the establishment of the Nicaean and the Comnene Empire of Trebizond. Secure in Konya, the new Sultan never forgot the obligation he was under to his Constantinopolitan friends and erstwhile hosts, and he took every opportunity to express his gratitude in a practical form. He did not hesitate to establish his Christian father-in-law in a fief on the Menander in Laodicaea,[22] and, at any rate to begin with, his sympathy for the Greeks led him to feel well-disposed towards Theodore Lascaris, though his inveterate dislike of the Latins and the Armenians remained as strong as ever. However, it was probably with the tacit approval of the Latin Emperor of Constantinople, Henry of Flanders, that he launched an attack on the port of Antalya, capturing it from the Aldobrandini in 1207. The acquisition of an outlet to the Mediterranean proved of immense benefit to the Seljukid economy, for the rapid expansion which had recently taken place in the country's trade made the possession of a port wellnigh essential. The western world was not slow to recognize the significance of the new development and to pay tribute to the Sultan's position as the head of a great commercial power by referring to Keyhüsrev's successor as '*Alatinus Magnus Soldanum Iconium et Potestas Omnium teararum per Orientem et Septentriondem, Plagam existentium et Magnus Cappadociae.*'[23]

However, Theodore Lascaris was perturbed and displeased by this development and his relations with Keyhüsrev deterior-ated. They became still more strained when Lascaris refused to cede his Nicaean empire to his father-in-law Alexios III, but

KEYHÜS-
REV I
1192–1196
AND
1204–1210

recently Emperor of Byzantium and now a penniless exile. Angered by this refusal Alexios appealed to Keyhüsrev, so lately his guest, for hospitality and help in obliging Lascaris to restore Nicaea. Mindful of the kindness the Emperor had shown him when he was himself an exile, the Seljuk accorded a warm welcome to the dispossessed monarch and wholeheartedly espoused his cause. He was all the readier to do so because Lascaris had recently annoyed him by entering into an alliance with Leo II of Armenia. War broke out between them in 1210, Lascaris's Greek troops being strengthened by the addition of Frankish, Bulgar and Hungarian units. Popular legend asserts that, in order to avoid heavy casualties, Keyhüsrev challenged Lascaris to settle the issue in single combat and that the Sultan was killed in the duel, but the historian Ibn Bibi[24] provides a different and more likely account of events. He relates that the battle was fought near Philadelphia (Alaşehir); in the course of it Lascaris was knocked from his horse and the Sultan's servants were about to strike him as he lay when Keyhüsrev intervened, helping Lascaris to remount and allowing him to depart.

Upon seeing Lascaris fall the Christian troops had fled, leading the Seljuks, who had fought splendidly, to conclude that they had won the battle. Dazzled by the prospect of capturing an immense booty the Turks forgot both duty and caution, and leaving their ruler unattended, they set off in pursuit of the enemy. A horseman chanced to ride past Keyhüsrev but the Sultan failed to realize that the man was a Frank and made no effort to protect himself. The rider on the other hand recognized the Sultan, and turning rapidly upon him, he pierced Keyhüsrev with his javelin and then set about despoiling the corpse, hoping to make off with his loot. An onlooker hurried to inform Lascaris of the deed. Lascaris ordered the Frank to be brought before him together with the body of the slain man. On recognizing the corpse he wept, then he commanded the

Frank to be put to death and gave instructions for the Sultan's body to be embalmed by a Muslim from Alaşehir in accordance with the Muhammadan rite and given honourable burial in the town's Muslim cemetery. Meanwhile, news of the Sultan's death had reached the Turkish camp, and in the general consternation which followed Lascaris was able to wrest from the Seljuks the victory which they had won in the fighting. Neither was Alexios, the cause of the war, to escape to continue the struggle; the Emperor's son-in-law was devoid of compassion and showed no hesitation in condemning the deposed ruler to life imprisonment in a Nicaean monastery. Then he turned northward, to lead his men towards the Black Sea.

Keyhüsrev was succeeded by his son Izzeddin, who assumed the title of Keykâvus I. According to Ibn Bibi, the new ruler was both a good and a handsome man; he was also a brave one and though peace-loving by temperament, and devoted to the arts, he was obliged to spend much of his time in warfare. He was a dutiful and also a devoted son, and one of his first acts as sovereign was to arrange for the re-burial of his father's body at Konya. Many difficulties marked the opening years of his reign, for although he had been elected to the throne by a group of powerful emirs, his right to it was contested both by his uncle Tügrül of Erzurum and by his younger brother, the future Keykûbad I. However, by 1213, he had dealt with both by strangling his uncle and imprisoning his brother. KEYKÂVUS I 1210/11– 1219

Next he turned to the pressing commercial problems, since trade now supplied the State with the greater part of its very considerable revenue. The Seljuks had by then enjoyed control of Antalya for just long enough for them to have learnt to appreciate the benefits they derived from it, but the port had recently been retaken by the Franks. In the east the political situation had also deteriorated, for Leo II of Armenia had availed himself of the opportunity offered by Keyhüsrev's death to recapture Eregli and Karaman, while in the north Lascaris had taken possession of the south-eastern section of the Black Sea coastline.

After recapturing Antalya (1214/15) and inflicting punish-ment on Leo II, Keykâvus next applied himself to securing outlets to the Black Sea, whence a lucrative transit trade be-tween China, India and Persia on the one hand and the West-ern world on the other could be developed, and at the same time a new offensive could be launched against Lascaris. Taking personal command of this army, Keykâvus captured Sinop late in 1214, and also managed to take prisoner Alexios Comnenos, Emperor of Trebizond, whilst the latter was on a hunting expedition. Wisely, he soon released his royal prisoner, having first made him accept the ties of vassaldom. He also at about this time celebrated his marriage to the daughter of the Emir of Erzincan.

Then in 1216 he turned east again, to expel Leo from Asia Minor. Having made him withdraw to Little Armenia, Keykâvus marched south, hoping to wrest Aleppo from Saladin's deputy; however, he died of consumption in 1219.

Though Keykâvus' reign had lasted for only a decade, he left his kingdom in a state of enviable prosperity, with Konya widely renowned as the capital of a realm the stability of which was based on the sound foundations provided by a strong, well-disciplined army, an efficient and loyal administration and a flourishing trade. In Anatolia many Seljuks were now fol-lowing sedentary occupations, agriculture was prospering, and wealth flowing into the provincial towns along the great high-ways which the Seljuks had made safe and efficient. With the Byzantines wholly engrossed in preserving what little they could from the depredations of the Crusaders, with the Emperor of Nicaea at war with the Franks, and with no Turkish emirs of any real importance to contend against, the future seemed full of promise for the next occupant of the throne.

Keykâvus's emirs decided to bestow the crown on Alaeddin, KEYKÛBAD I
releasing him from confinement that he might succeed his   1219–1236
brother as Keykûbad I. The new ruler was to prove the greatest
of his dynasty. His talents were varied and of a high order,
and it may have been during his imprisonment that he became
an excellent calligrapher and draughtsman, a good carpenter
and a skilled maker of bows. He showed himself a wise and
efficient administrator, bringing prosperity back to the districts
which had been so bitterly fought over by his predecessors,
embellishing Konya beyond all recognition, and developing
Sivas into one of the most important trading cities of the Levant.
He was also an excellent military leader and was able within
twelve months of his accession to capture Kalonoros (Alaiye)
from the Armenians, and to transform it into a naval base the
like of which was not to be found anywhere in the Mediterranean. Not satisfied with this, he turned much of Anatolia
into a market garden, and encouraged industrial developments
such as the building of sugar refineries, notably in the hinter-
land of Alaiye.

In the fifteen years of Keykûbad's reign his armies covered   DESTRUC-
themselves with glory. Though the Genoese tried to debar the   TION OF
Seljuks from benefiting from their conquest of Sinop, Keykû-   KWARAZM
bad embarked from this port in the first year of his reign to lead
a punitive expedition across the Black Sea to Sudak. In 1222
his nephew, the governor of Sinop, involved the Sultanate in
an unprofitable war against the Emperor of Trebizond; while
it was taking place Keykûbad steadily cleared the western
Taurus as far as Silivke of Armenians, till he had gained the
submission of the whole of Lesser Armenia. Its collapse
brought the Sultan into direct conflict with Celaleddin of
Kwarazm,[25] who had extended his boundary to include Ahlat.
In 1230, with the aid of the Eyubite Prince al Aşraf,
Keykûbad attacked this powerful rival and inflicted so severe

a defeat on the Kwarazmian Shah at Erzincan that it amounted to a triumph. The victory, however, contained a hidden sting, only to become apparent later; even at the time, though it won the Sultan widespread fame, it served to arouse the jealousy and dread of Keykûbad's ally. The latter now busied himself in rallying sixteen Eyubite princes of Egypt and Iraq, who agreed to march into Asia Minor under the command of Malık al Kamıl of Egypt. Thus while still pursuing his war against Kwarazm, Keykûbad had to divert troops to meet the new threat. However, his men once again proved their superiority by recapturing, if only temporarily, Harput, Harran and Rakka, thus leaving their sovereign free to advance into the kingdom of Kwarazm till he had completely subjugated it.

Kwarazm had for centuries served as a buffer state between the cultured dynasties which had replaced the earlier civilizations of the ancient Orient and the turbulent nomads roaming the Eurasian plain. Though its removal brought fame to Keykûbad, its collapse was in the long run to prove disastrous not only to the Sultanate of Rum, but likewise to Persia and Iraq; at the time no one realized that the victory was a barren one and Keykûbad was perhaps not unfortunate in dying when he did, even though death came to him in the form of poison, said to have been administered at the order of his son. By this vile act the latter inherited in 1235/36 a kingdom which comprised the whole of Asia Minor with the exception of the Comnene kingdom of Trebizond and the Vatatze lands of Lesser Armenia, though both these recognized the Seljuks as their suzerains, Trebizond having renewed her bond when Kwarazm collapsed, in punishment for affording sanctuary to a number of Kwarazmian soldiers.

KEYHÜSREV
II
1236–1246

The new ruler, Giyaseddin, adopted the title of Keyhüsrev II. He was of a light-hearted disposition, and like many of his Persian contemporaries, he delighted in the cup of wine and its accompanying songs and pithy quatrains. On ascending the throne he married his sister to the Eyubite Prince Melik Aziz, the son of Muhammad, ruler of Aleppo, and he himself married the latter's daughter; but soon after, he fell passionately in love, and married as his second wife the Princess Russudana, daughter of the Georgian Queen, Tamara, treating her in all respects as his consort.

Though Keyhüsrev II had inherited an immensely valuable empire, in Central Asia the tribes had for some years past been on the move again. On this occasion it was the Mongols who were on the march and, as they penetrated westward, marking their advance by a series of actions of unimaginable cruelty, terror spread among the peaceful inhabitants of the neighbouring lands. Each new rumour or report concerning the Mongols fanned their fears, till at last hordes of panic-stricken refugees fled, abandoning their homes and fields to the invaders. The number of the emigrants was swelled by numerous ne'er-do-wells, potential criminals mingling with harmless peasants, lawless dervishes with timid pilgrims. Many broke through into the Sultanate of Rum where the very sight of the rabble terrified the inhabitants, whose apprehension increased even further as dervish orators came forward to incite both the refugees and the local peasantry to rebellion. Many of the dervishes had in fact abandoned their calling to become political agitators, who did not hesitate to further their cause by ascribing the Sultan's willingness to grant trading concessions to foreign merchants to a preference for Christians. These reports helped to aggravate the distrust, and the unrest soon became so widespread that the Sultan was forced to rely on Christian mercenaries in his army rather than on his subjects, a situation which in its turn added fresh substance to the flood of pernicious rumours.

At first, perhaps deterred by the military renown of the Seljuks, the bulk of the Mongol forces invaded and conquered southern

THE
MONGOL
THREAT

73

Russia. Some of them settled on the lower reaches of the Volga and the Don to form the kingdom of the Golden Horde, whilst others established themselves as suzerains of the Kievian prin- cipality. Meanwhile, realizing that the disappearance of the kingdom of Kwarazm had greatly facilitated their entry into Persia, another wave of Mongols overran that country and made themselves masters of Baghdad. Even in Keykûbad's lifetime others had begun to feel their way into Asia Minor; with his death they accelerated their pace and in doing so, they dislodged some of the Turkish tribes which had recently settled along the eastern boundaries of Rum. Among the uprooted Ghuzz nomads were the Kayi people, who were to go down to history as the Osmanlis. Their chieftain Süleyman led them into Asia Minor. Legend relates that one day Tügrül, Süley- man's son and successor, saw two bands of horsemen engaged in a fierce contest. Pausing just long enough to ascertain which of the two was the weaker, Tügrül rallied his men and rushed to their aid. His arrival proved opportune for it tipped the scales in favour of no less a person than the Seljukid Sultan and his bodyguard who had been set upon by a band of Mongols. Keyhüsrev's gratitude was profound and he expressed it by presenting Tügrül with a strip of land in the Karaçadag. The fief stretched from Eskişehir almost to Konya; it included Söğüt and Domaniç, and it was at Söğüt that Tügrül's son Osman was born and, in 1324, buried.

BATTLE OF KUZADAG In 1241/42 the Mongols besieged and captured Erzurum. Their approach convinced Keyhüsrev that it was now only a matter of time before he would himself have to confront the invaders in battle and he set about assembling his troops. He collected some 70,000 men and placed them under the com- mand of a Georgian general, a Prince Shervashidze.[26] The Mongolian army was rather smaller; it was commanded by Baidju, and likewise included a number of Georgian and

Armenian mercenaries. The two forces engaged in battle on the morning of 26th June 1242, at a point on the Sivas to Erzincan road close to Kuzadag. Shervashidze was killed in the fighting, and, on hearing the news, the Seljukid soldiers who had emerged victorious from so many great engagements against powerful enemies of diverse nationalities crumbled in the face of the overwhelming ferocity of the Mongol onslaught.

The Seljuks fled, abandoning their camp with the coloured tents of their notables, leaving even their Sultan's tent and his personal standard bearing a lion straining at its leash to fall to their conquerors. The Mongols went on to plunder Tokat and Kayseri, and Keyhüsrev escaped to Konya, leaving two loyal subjects, the Emir Mudhahibeddin and the Cadi of Amasya, to negotiate the peace terms. The Sultan's hopes of persuading Baldwin II to enter into an alliance against the Mongols proved vain, and he had to accept the bonds of vassalship in return for the retention of but nominal power.

Panic spread throughout Anatolia at the news of the Mongolian victory; once again the fields of Asia Minor were left untilled in the face of the enemy's advance, famine broke out in the land, and hordes of wealthy Seljuks appeared, anxiously trying to exchange magnificent jewels for a morsel of food. Some of the minor Turkish chieftains sought to secure their strips of land by marrying their daughters to Mongolian notables; others swept into Paphlagonia and Pamphilia in search of safety. Turcoman nomads appeared to sack the Seljukid cities and the general disorganization became so great that, in 1246, it affected court circles and a band of notables rising in revolt strangled their defenceless sovereign. Then a pretender appeared to claim the vacant throne, affirming that he was a son of Keykûbad I. He succeeded in rallying some twenty thousand men to his standard, but he was finally caught and hanged at Alaiye.[27]

PERIOD OF
ANARCHY

The Mongol ruler Hulagu soon realized that the Turcoman rising could rapidly become dangerous and so instructed Izzed-din Keykâvus II, the late Sultan's eldest son and successor, to restore order, and capture and punish the leaders. Izzeddin suc-ceeded in this to some extent, but other Turkish and Turcoman chieftains quickly appeared in the under-manned provinces to assume the powers of autonomous princelings, and his brother Ruknûddin rose against him at Sivas. Annoyed by this new development, Hulagu decided that all three brothers were to share the throne. It was largely owing to the ability of the Grand Vizir, Şemseddin Juwaini of Isfahan, that the trium-virate endured for eleven years, but these years were marked by constant plotting and intrigue, mercenaries enrolling first in one camp then in the other. To complicate matters further, at one point the Byzantine Emperor Michael, fearing the jealousy of Theodore II of Nicaea, sought refuge with Izzeddin at Konya and was appointed by the Sultan commander of his Christian mercenaries.[28] The decision was not a popular one, for it made the people doubt Izzeddin's devotion to the Muslim religion, reminding them of the fact that his mother had been a Chris-tian. This helped to add substance to the report that the Sultan had gone over to his mother's faith, a rumour which gained in credibility when, in the course of the trial of the Greek Patriarch Anthemius, the Emperor Michael charged the prelate with showing excessive partiality to the Seljuks.[29] Ruknûddin, the second of the three brothers, took advantage of these suspicions to quarrel with Izzeddin, who, however, contrived to imprison him.

The affair angered the great Batu and Izzeddin hurriedly released Ruknûddin; then the two brothers decided to send Alaeddin, the youngest of the trio, to the Mongolian court to placate Batu. It was there that Friar Rubruquis saw him, but it is probable that the young Sultan died on his return journey, for no more is heard of him after the year 1257, at about the

THE TRIUM-VIRATE
1246–1257

time when Mangu gave orders that Izzeddin was to rule over
Seljukid lands lying to the east of the Halys, and Ruknûddin
over those to the west of it. Izzeddin considered that the decision favoured Ruknûddin and menaced his own safety, and
he therefore conspired with the Mamluks of Egypt to overthrow
his Mongol suzerain. The Mongolian viceroy of Asia Minor
soon learnt of the plot and set out to chastise Izzeddin; but the
latter was in his turn warned by a friend and hastily assembling
his family, he set out for Antalya, proceeding thence to Sardis
to invoke the help of Theodore II Lascaris. Failing to obtain it,
Izzeddin gratefully accepted the invitation of the Byzantine
Emperor to seek sanctuary at his court, an offer made in return
for the hospitality which the Greek had himself so recently
received from the Seljuk.

Leaving Ruknûddin sole governor of what remained of the   IZZEDDIN
Seljukid empire, Izzeddin reached Constantinople in 1261,   1246–1283?
probably entering the city in the Emperor's train on the town's
liberation from the Latins. There he was treated graciously,
and even permitted to wear the purple slippers that served the
Byzantines as an emblem of royalty. But the Emperor was himself greatly afraid of the Mongols, and within a few months,
forgetful of his duties as a host, he attempted to ensure the
safety of his realm by imprisoning Izzeddin and two of his sons
in the fortress of Eros, and then asking the Mongols to reward
him for the deed by a promise of immunity. It may well have
been the fear of some such development that induced Izzeddin,
some time before 1263, to conspire with the Bulgarian sovereign
Constantine Tish against his imperial host.[30] There are various
versions of the events which followed both these moves,[31] but
it would seem that eventually Izzeddin, together with his
eldest son and possibly another son, were rescued by Barkay,
Khan of the Djuci tribe of the Crimean Tartars, a connection
by marriage, who advanced on Constantinople for the purpose.

By the year 1263/64 the ex-Sultan and his son Mesud were in Serai in the Crimea, the capital of Barkay.[32] Some authorities state that Izzeddin had tried to persuade his men to accompany him across the Black Sea, but that they refused, preferring to enrol in the Byzantine army where, on being promised that they would never be asked to take up arms against their kins-men, they formed the corps of the Turcopoles; but even then not all agreed to serve the Emperor. Some Seljuks made their way to the Dobrudja, to survive there into modern times as a tiny community known as the Gagauz, a name which Wittek regards as a corruption of Keykâvus, Izzeddin having adopted the latter as his royal title. Still others fled to Serbia where, in 1308, King Milutin gave them a strip of land on which to settle.[33] Some of these revolted and set out to seek employment as mercenaries with the Franks of the Morea as well as with the Serbs, the Bulgars, the Greeks of Epirus, and the Byzantines. Many became Christians. Izzeddin's youngest son was among the converts, and remained in Constantinople after his father's flight, eventually marrying a Greek girl there.[34]

Barkay treated Izzeddin kindly and talked of establishing him on an estate of his own; but the old Khan died before he had had time to fulfil this undertaking and his son and succes-sor acted very differently, imprisoning Izzeddin and Mesud in a small village on the shore of the Black Sea. After about eight years, in about 1283, Izzeddin died there but Mesud managed to escape. He made his way back to the Mongolian court where he petitioned his suzerain to restore him to his father's throne. His wish was partially granted for he was given the eastern half of the Sultanate to rule, while his cousin Alaeddin Keykûbad III was allowed to retain control over the western portion.

KILIÇAR-
SLAN IV
1246–1264

When Izzeddin fled from Konya in 1260 his brother Ruk-nûddin automatically became sole ruler of Rum under the title of Kılıçarslan IV, yet he reigned as a vassal, almost as a puppet of the Mongols, and even the little authority which remained vested in him actually rested in the hands of his powerful Prime Minister, the Pervane Muin ed din Süleyman. The Mongols encouraged the Pervane to become all-powerful, conferring upon him the additional office of Cadi or Supreme Judge, an appointment which greatly angered the local princes. Nevertheless, at Ruknûddin's murder at Aksaray in 1264—a deed which some people ascribe to the Pervane—the minister raised the late sovereign's son Giyaseddin Keyhüsrev III to the throne. As the boy was still an infant the Mongolian Ilkhan remained the virtual ruler of the kingdom, the day-to-day control of affairs being left to the Pervane.

For ten years the Pervane administered the kingdom wisely and loyally; then, as Giyaseddin approached manhood and independence, the canker of envy entered his heart, inducing him to enter into a conspiracy with Baibars, the Mamluk Sultan of Egypt. Together they plotted to evict the Mongols from Asia Minor and to raise the Pervane to the Seljukid throne. At first all went according to plan: in 1276/77 they defeated the Mongols at Elbistan and entered Konya; then, as they regrouped at Kayseri for further battle, the Pervane took fright; his fear communicated itself to the Mamluk who hurriedly withdrew to Egypt, leaving the Pervane to be put to death in the following year by his angry Mongolian suzerain.

Giyaseddin Keyhüsrev III, though aged only fifteen, now assumed sovereign power. His position was extremely difficult, for the covetous local Turkish atabegs, encouraged by the Pervane's fall, took advantage of his inexperience to establish themselves as well-nigh autocratic rulers in many parts of the kingdom. Even the late Pervane's own sons could not resist installing themselves at Sinop, as did members of the household of the late Vizir Sahip Ata at Afion Kara Hisar. It was with real pleasure, therefore, that the young sovereign watched

Osman, son of Tügrül, who had succeeded to the chieftainship of the Osmanli tribe, harass the Byzantines, in 1281 extending his fief at their expense. Keyhüsrev marked the occasion by investing him with the title of Üç Beg, meaning Protector of the Border, giving him the drum and horse-hair standard consisting of a red pennant with a white crescent upon it[35] which accompanied the title; it may also have been on this occasion that the Seljuk made the future founder of the Ottoman dynasty the gift of the robe which is recorded in surviving documents.[36]

At his death in 1283 Keyhüsrev III was succeeded by his nephew Alaeddin Keykûbad III, the son of his brother Faremurz; but almost immediately, the new sovereign was obliged to cede the eastern half of his kingdom to his cousin Mesud II. Mesud died in 1298. He was succeeded by his son Mesud III, who spent his time contending against Keykûbad III for full sovereignty; the quarrel continued when Giyaseddin succeeded his father Keykûbad in 1302, lasting till 1308, when Mesud's death by murder in Kayseri settled the issue. It is doubtful whether Giyaseddin survived him for any length of time, for his name disappears from history very soon after, and with it ends the history of the Seljuks of Rum.

CHAPTER III

The Seljukid Way of Life

THE GREAT SELJUKS retained many usages and tastes dating from their nomadic days, but they adjusted them to the principal tenets of their new faith and increased them by the addition of a number of Persian customs and beliefs. The Seljuks of Asia Minor superimposed on these certain Western, or rather, Byzantine habits, fusing the various elements into a surprisingly homogeneous and strongly individualistic way of life. Thus, although the basic pattern continued to conform to the needs and ideals of a race of warriors, its outer facets assumed numerous more complex and stimulating forms.

The Sultanate of Rum, like the Empire of the Great Seljuks, was an essentially military state and the efficiency of the army always remained a matter of supreme importance. Alp Arslan and Malık Shah had been glad to entrust the organization of the military machine to the Nizam al Mulk. Mindful of the old tribal ties which continued to bind the men to their chieftains, the Vizir divided the kingdom into twenty-four sections, each of which he placed in the care of a commander whose title varied from the Chad of the Ghuzz tribal society to the Persian Shah or the Mongol Khan, which reached the Seljuks by means of the Avars.[37] These chieftains were charged with the duty of raising annually a specific number of recruits and equipping them with arms.

Each spring the seasoned soldiers and the raw recruits assembled in the presence of their sovereign, at a rallying point indicated in the summons sent out in the Sultan's name. The men spent the summer months either training or campaigning, dispersing in the winter when bad weather made fighting impossible. For a time this method of recruitment sufficed to meet the country's needs, but all too soon it became necessary to augment it, first by levying trained men as a form of tribute, then by enrolling mercenaries into the army.

The soldiers were hardened off each spring in tough training schools where much attention was paid to turning them into excellent horsemen and splendid shots, dexterity in archery and fencing forming part of their basic training. All were encour/ aged to take part in games of skill, and they were expected to play polo at least once a week.[38] At a later stage the men were split up into groups, some of which were sent for instruction in the use of the spear and sword, while others, the best, were drafted into the cavalry, which formed the most important branch of the army. Many of the soldiers wore chain mail and pointed helms; all carried shields, and many of the officers used swords. Some of these were double/bladed, and a good many were mounted into handles ending in the two/lobed leaf ter/ minal, which is a characteristic feature of Seljukid decoration.

Plate 61

Fig. 3

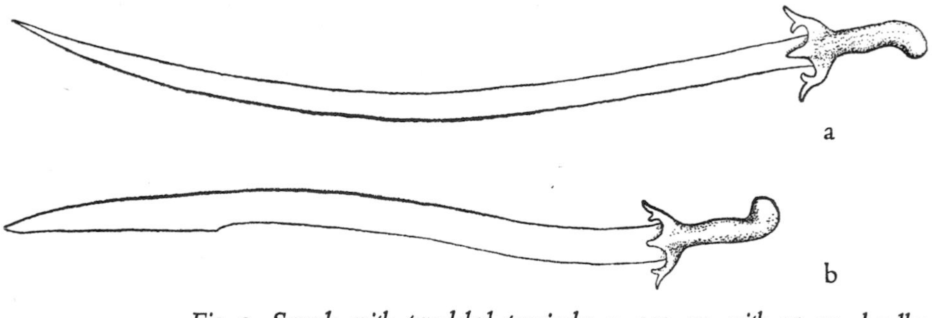

a

b

Fig. 3. Swords with two/lobed terminals: a. 100 cm. with 15 cm. handle; b. 85 cm. with 16 cm. handle.

The archers were provided with notched arrows, which had often been dipped in poison.

To mark the opening of the campaigning season the sultans of Rum would hold a review of their troops. Kayseri was often chosen for the event, which was popular among the men since the parade was always followed by much feasting, enlivened by displays of horsemanship and entertainments by jugglers and acrobats, who walked among the guests performing feats of skill and agility. Bards chanted their epics, poets recited their latest compositions and musicians such as lute players, harpists, pipers and drummers provided musical interludes.

Although the Great Seljuks had not hesitated to divest the Caliph of his temporal powers, they continued to honour and uphold his spiritual authority, loudly proclaiming themselves his champions and protectors, and, indeed, always holding themselves ready to support this claim by the force of their arms. Every Seljuk felt that he shared in the obligation, yet notwithstanding his respect for and devotion to the Caliph, each looked upon the Sultan as his supreme master, and throughout the dominion the feeling of personal loyalty to the dynasty was so strong that, with the single exception of the Pervane Muin ed din, there is no instance of an attempt being made to usurp the royal powers by anyone outside the circle of the sovereign's heirs. Some local princes were permitted to use the title of shah, but that of shahanshah or sultan was reserved for the supreme sovereign and none but the Buyids ever ventured to usurp the privilege.

THE MONARCHY

In Seljukid times it was the custom for the crown to pass from father to son, generally going to the eldest, though occasionally a member of the royal family would attempt to revive the old Ghuzz practice whereby, as in Kievian Russia, kingship passed to the dead ruler's eldest surviving brother and not to his first-born son. On such occasions the issue was settled by force, the throne going to the strongest claimant.

In Persia, at the death of Malık Shah, the weakened central authority could no longer exercise complete control over its vassals, and many of these developed into autocratic chiefs ruling over considerable provinces. Some assumed the title of 'atabeg', that is to say 'father prince', not caring that the rank had been especially created by Alp Arslan for the Nizam al Mulk when the latter was appointed tutor to the young Malik Shah. Subsequent sultans also considered the title the special prerogative of the holder of the office of tutor to the heir apparent, a post which was invariably assigned to the sovereign's most trusted minister of state. Even during the closing decades of the empire's existence, at a time when minor chieftains were assuming titles to which they had no right, the Seljukid sultans were reluctant to accord this honour to any courtiers other than their vizirs. One of the last occasions on which it was fittingly bestowed was when Keykûbad II conferred it on his Cadi or Chief Justice to mark his elevation to the vizirship; that the minister was worthy of the honour was proved by his death in defence of his sovereign in an encounter with the Mongols.[39]

MINIS
TERIAL
DUTIES AND
RANKS

In the 13th century the Seljuks vested the functions of the *Vizir* or Prime Minister in the *Pervane* or Lord Chancellor, who also automatically held the office of President of the Council or *Divan*. As his sovereign's representative he was responsible for all internal affairs and, in the Sultan's absence, it fell to him to preside at the meetings of the cabinet. The Commander-in-Chief ranked second in the order of precedence. He was followed by the *Cadi* or Chief Justice, who generally came from Baghdad and who, since the Seljukid legal code was based on the Koran, either combined the post with that of Chief *Mufti*, the supreme religious authority, or shared his place in the order of precedence with the prelate, when both generally acted jointly in the administrative field. When the offices were combined, the Cadi's prestige in Asia Minor was almost as great as that enjoyed by the Sheikh al Islam in the Muslim world.

Nevertheless, it was to the sultan and not the ministers that the people looked for religious inspiration; in Alaeddin Keykûbad I they found a splendid source for it. His fervour was deep and passionate, his reverence profound. He was in the habit of reading daily the morning prayer of the *Shafia* and the five prayers of the *Hanifa*,[40] and he made a particular point of performing his ablutions before signing the daily edicts of the Divan because the name of Allah appeared in the documents which were submitted to him. The emirs in charge of various branches of the army followed the Chief Cadi and the Mufti in the order of precedence. These officials formed the inner cabinet, but a number of senior notables and tribal begs or princes joined them in attending the meetings of the Divan, acting as a sort of consultative body.

In the early days of the Great Seljukid empire the officials who formed the country's government used to meet in the *Kapu* or entrance to their sovereign's tent, assembling there as had their tribal forebears in that of their chieftain. When the committee, following the practice in force at the Sasanian court, moved from the doorway into the hall within, the ministers then seating themselves on the divans set round its walls, the Seljuks continued to call the meeting-place by the old name of Kapu. The designation was retained by the Ottoman rulers of the Turkish empire, whose council hall was known as the *Sublime Porte* and where the actual assembly continued to be called by the old Sasanian name of the Divan.

THE DIVAN AND THE PORTE

In the Sultanate of Rum the work of the Divan was carried out by twenty-four secretaries, half of whom were concerned with military matters while the rest dealt with financial affairs. The Vizir or Pervane, wearing the ink pot presented to him on his appointment by the Sultan as his badge of office, took sole responsibility for the country's foreign affairs; the necessary correspondence and records were entrusted by him to a special body of scribes who, although they occasionally made use of Arabic, generally carried out their work in the Persian language. All state papers were usually written in the *viahat* or dotless script, and all carried the Sultan's seal. Under the Mongol occupation the Turkish language was introduced into the chancelleries, where it soon came to be accepted as the official tongue. The Sultan's personal wishes were invariably recorded in writing, either from his direct dictation or from verbal instructions, when the messengers were expected to display the Sultan's ring as proof of authenticity. The royal commands were written on special paper reserved for the purpose; it was white, exceptionally fine-textured, and was probably imported from China.

SECRET POLICE

The Seljukid sultans were extremely devout and, taken by and large, all strove to live righteously and to rule wisely and well. The Ummayads and the Abbasids had established a secret police service; it was run by a *Sahib-haras*, and it was the duty of the men employed in it to keep watch on political suspects and to execute those whom the caliphs condemned to death. The system was repulsive to Alp Arslan who, against the advice of the Nizam, determined to abolish it, saying, should 'I appoint a Sahib-khaban, those who are my sincere friends and enjoy my intimacy will not pay any attention to him, nor bribe him, trusting in their fidelity, friendship and intimacy. On the other hand my adversaries and enemies will make friends with him and give him money; it is clear that the Sahib-khaban will be constantly bringing me bad reports of my friends and good reports of my enemies. Good and evil words are like arrows; if several are shot, at least one hits the target. Every day my sympathy for my friends will diminish and that for my enemies increase. Within a short time my enemies will be nearer to me than my friends and will finally take their place. No one will be able to repair the harm which will result from this.'[41]

These were wise words, yet, in Persia, they did not save the Seljukid administration from all friction with the native population. A good many difficulties resulted from the inevitable distrust with which the sophisticated Persians regarded the wild Seljukid rank and file. Though these were the men by whom the cultured Persians had been vanquished, the latter wished to see the same treatment meted out to them by their sovereign as they themselves received as a subjected people; when they found that this was asking too much from the Sultan, the Persians demanded that the Seljukid soldiers be treated as the equals of the mercenaries and slaves enrolled in the Sultan's army.

Naturally enough, neither proposal proved acceptable to the conquerors, all of whom considered themselves linked to their ruler by tribal ties and insisted on their privileges. An attempt to bring the two groups closer together by giving the Seljukid soldiers a Persian veneer did little to diminish the friction, for the average Seljuk continued to prefer his own austere customs to the seemingly effete manners of the Persians. Indeed, with the years the cleavage tended to become more marked, for the sovereigns gradually became more urbane and luxury-loving while the tribesmen did not alter. The displeasure which they felt when Malık Shah, in direct disregard of the Nizam's advice, ceased to devote much of his attention to the army, and began to appoint one person to several posts at court, helped to spread the Ismaili doctrines and lost the sultans much support of which they were soon to be in sore need.

The Seljuks were generally ready to fall in with local conditions as long as these did not conflict with the tenets of their faith. On conquering Asia Minor, once the initial phase of plunder and murder had run its course, they showed little desire deliberately to disrupt the life of the people, endeavouring to retain existing laws and customs, readily accepting the regulations they found there concerning the tenure of land. Where they considered changes necessary they adopted whenever possible measures similar to those which the Great Seljuks had introduced POLICY IN CONQUERED LANDS in Persia. The most important of their reforms were concerned with legislation. Murder was punishable by death, but it could sometimes be commuted on the payment of blood money. When the sentence was carried out the condemned person was either strangled, hanged or beheaded, but in the direst cases, the victim was skinned alive, the skin being turned into an effigy which was carried round the town before being placed in a hut specially constructed for the purpose and publicly burnt. Less serious crimes were punished by exile or by public thrashings, or even by the confiscation of property.

CORONA⁄TIONS

Coronations were popular events. On the throne falling vacant the new sovereign was met by the religious and civil authorities carrying gold cups filled with honey and mares' milk, while other officials went through the town distributing vast sums of money. With the passing years the Sultans forgot the simple customs of their tribal ancestors, and developed instead a pre⁄ference for the Persian concept of autocratic sovereignty, as well as a liking for the voluptuous habits of Baghdad and the luxurious ways of the Byzantines. Though Kılıçarslan II pre⁄ferred to rule his people in the paternal manner of a tribal chief⁄tain, his successors wished to govern in the style of a Persian monarch. As in Persia, they had themselves carried to their throne, where gold and silver were showered upon them. In

Fig. 4

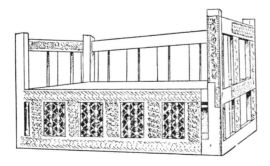

Fig. 4. Wooden throne of Keyhüsrev III (1264–1283) from the Kızıl Bey Cami. Length 1 m. 25 cm.; width, 1 m. 21 cm.; height, 1 m. 56 cm.

Persia, under the Nizam, the Sultan had been provided with an escort made up of two hundred men from Horasan, a hundred from Dailan and a company of Christian slaves.[42] The latter proved so fanatically loyal to their sovereign that they were soon used to form the nucleus of his personal body‑guard and, as such, may well have given the Sultans of Ottoman Turkey the idea of creating their Janissary corps.

When taking part in a procession the Sultan was preceded by his standard bearer carrying the imperial banner; this had a black ground and displayed either the figure of a dragon, the choice of which can be attributed to either Chinese or Sasanian influence, of a lion, the origin of which can be traced back to the old civilizations of the Ancient Orient, or of an eagle, in which case the influence may have been that of Byzantium, though it could equally well have come from Central Asia or even Persia. In the closing period the Sultan was also preceded by an attendant carrying an open umbrella in the manner of his Fatimid arch‑enemies; on either side of him marched a detachment of foot soldiers carrying golden swords.[43]

Coronations, great military successes and other occasions for FESTIVITIES national rejoicing were celebrated in the traditional manner, feasting and various entertainments providing the chief diver‑ sions. Both ibn Batuta and ibn Bibi state that the Sultan's board was dressed at a high table, and his guests were placed at it according to a strict order of precedence. Vast quantities of lamb, goat meat, game and pigeons were served on precious dishes elaborately ornamented and bejewelled. Sherbet was handed round in costly cups by sumptuously‑dressed servants, many of whom were Christian slaves. On state occasions a general amnesty was often proclaimed and the prison doors were opened at dawn so that the released men could share in the celebrations. The festivities were similar to those organized at the annual military review, but plays and puppet shows were included in the entertainments. Anna Comnena[44] gives us some idea of what these performances were like in her account of the preparations by Alexios to launch an assault on Sivas.

He had, however, to postpone operations because of an acute attack of gout. The Seljukid soldiers questioned his reason, crediting the Emperor with a diplomatic rather than a physical ailment. They joked about it 'when drunk or drinking and, as natural orators, the barbarians told moral tales about the Emperor's sufferings in his feet, and the trouble in his feet became the subject of comedies. For they would impersonate doctors and other people busied about the Emperor and place the Emperor himself in the middle, lying on a couch, and make play of it. And these puerile games aroused much laughter among the barbarians. These doings did not escape the Emperor and they made him boil with anger, and provoked him still more to war with them.'

COURT CIRCLES The new, relaxing way of life inevitably resulted in the Sultan becoming to some extent estranged from the rank and file of his people. The gap was filled by the emergence of a new class consisting of courtiers and officials. Appointments to these offices were often dictated by the Sultan's personal wishes, but when he failed to show a preference for any particular person the officer was selected by means of the ancient oriental custom whereby all the candidates were assembled before the Sultan and his court, and made to discourse on certain specific topics. Even the Pervane Muin ed din resorted to this method on more than one occasion. The ablest and wisest dialectician was nominated to the vacant post. The Sultan generally invested him with the title of beg, but sometimes he would confer on him a Persian or Byzantine honour instead, for the Seljuks delighted in titles of every sort, awarding them regardless of origin or suitability, in much the same spirit as that in which Kılıçarslan II blithely called one of his sons Müiseddin Kaiser Shah.

The Master of Ceremonies was among the most important of the court officials, but the Master of the Water was almost his equal in rank. This official had to ensure an unfailing supply of water, and above all, of good drinking water for the royal table, since the Seljuks, like all Turks, even those of today, attached as much importance to the quality of their drinking water as Frenchmen do to that of their wine. His post was no sinecure, for periods of drought and difficulties of transport had to be contended with, and unexpected problems often arose to complicate the task; thus, when Izzeddin Keykâvus I was taken ill at Kirşehir the Master of the Water was obliged to provide drinking water from the Euphrates, though the distance over which it had to be carried amounted to a hundred and fifty miles. Almost as important to the Sultan as these functionaries was his personal doctor. Like ibn Batuta of Birge, who held the post for many years, this official was often a Jew.

Even though the royal family retained the loyalty and devotion of its people till well into the Mongol period, the creation of this class of courtiers inevitably resulted in the growth of intrigue, which in its turn led to that of political conspiracy. Because of this it became necessary for the later Seljukid sultans to disregard Alp Arslan's brave decision and to create the post of Taster of Food and Drink. Even so, more than one sovereign died unexpectedly, and the mystery associated with their deaths gave rise to a spate of rumours.

The position of Seljukid women deteriorated with the tribe's development into a monarchy. In the pagan, nomadic period of their history they had not ranked as greatly inferior to their menfolk; they had gone unveiled and had fought in battle beside their fathers and husbands; but when the Seljuks were won over to Muhammadanism their women were expected to assume the veil and to retire to the seclusion of the harem. They

SELJUKID
WOMEN

were thenceforth debarred from taking part in their people's affairs, and were forced to spend their lives in the shadow of the momentous events which led to their rise and fall. Occasionally, however, a woman with a more forceful character than her sisters left her name to posterity by means of an inscription set upon the walls of some charitable institution erected at her order; more often, the fact of a woman's passage on this earth was somewhat ironically attested to by means of an in-scription placed upon her mausoleum to record her journey from a world of twilight to one of darkness. But the tendency of the sultans to take Christian women as their wives often led to very different results. Roxelana's excursions into the political field are well known; Isabella, the sister of Raymond of St Egidier and wife of Kılıçarslan I, must have kept a keen watch on affairs of state, for had she not done so she would scarcely have been in a position to install her son Tügrül as ruler of Malatya as soon as she learnt of her husband's death.

Giyaseddin Keyhüsrev II's Georgian wife, the Princess Russudana, who was known to the Seljuks as Göörgci Hatun, must also have exercised considerable influence over her hus-band. At the time of their marriage he was so much in love with her that, regardless of the exception which devout Mus-lims take to all forms of representational art, he is reputed to have wished to include her portrait beside his own on his coins; other authorities, however, state that he merely wanted their linked names to appear on them.[45] When public opposition forced him to abandon the idea, he carried out his intention by stamping the face of his coins with a rendering of the sun in Leo, choosing this emblem either because he wished it to symbolize his wife's radiant personality or because it represented her horoscope; he also included the figure of a lion in the design to represent his own person. This lion, with its outlines not greatly altered, survived in Persia into modern times, for Feth Ali Shah chose it as his country's crest.

Plates 79, 80

The readiness with which Christian parents gave their daughters in marriage to the Seljukid sultans suggests that these sultanas enjoyed certain privileges which were refused to Muslim women holding the same position. The greatest of these was assuredly their right to retain the religion of their birth with full opportunity for practising it, a concession which must have helped them to preserve their self-respect and independence of spirit. Of the Muslim women only the Princess Gevher Fevsi or Nesibi Hatun, known also as Seljuka Hatun, is recorded in history because of the great love which her father Kılıçarslan II felt for her.

Generally the Sultans found their wives in the various princely Turkish houses of the neighbourhood, such as those of the Danışmend rulers, of the Tzakas family or of the Begs of Erzincan. These ladies cannot have wielded much influence over their husbands, since the alliances did not mitigate the quarrels which raged between a Sultan and his father-in-law and which often ended in warfare. On becoming widows all the consorts, regardless of their religion or origin, were expected to marry one of the late Sultan's ministers of state. This custom was probably of nomadic origin, but it persisted in Asia Minor throughout the entire Seljukid period, and it was in accordance with it that Şemseddin Isfahani, the holder of the vizirship during the Triumvirate, married the widow of Giyaseddin Keyhüsrev II, the Georgian mother of Keykâvus II.

The burial customs of the Seljuks likewise reflected some alien BURIAL elements. Thus, certain authorities tend to ascribe the wearing CUSTOMS of black as a sign of mourning to Christian, and more specifically to Greek influence. If this is so the impact must have been made in early Islamic and not in Seljukid times, for the first recorded use of it for the purpose dates from the murder of Yehia in the year 742, when his followers donned black and the Abbasids adopted the colour for their flag.[46] When

Keykûbad I was brought to the throne in 1219, he wore white satin for three days as a sign of mourning for his brother.[47] In contrast, the habit of the Mevlevi Dervishes of including pipe players in their funeral processions may well be of Western origin.

Apart from these alien elements, the basically Muslim ritual also included certain features which, notwithstanding considerable modification brought about by the passage of the years and the changes in environment, remained essentially Central Asian. Although very little is known as yet about the burial customs of the Ghuzz some early Chinese writers clearly indicate that they venerated their dead. The Muslim religion does not share nor approve of this attitude, yet, throughout their history, the Seljuks continued to attach great importance to the graves of their ancestors. They were encouraged to continue this nomadic custom by the Shi'ite Persians, or rather, by the Suni Turkish rulers of Shi'ite Persia, whose great funerary towers and monuments are still a glorious adornment of the Persian landscape. The Seljuks in their turn persisted in the habit of constructing *türbes* and *kümbets*—the domed and pinnacle-roofed mausolea—which became so characteristic a feature of their architecture.

Barthold noted with interest[48] that the belief recorded in the Orkhon inscriptions, that on leaving the body the soul of a dead person turns into a bird or insect, continued to be reflected in modern times in the speech of the Ottoman Turks, who often announced a death in the phrase 'he has become a gire-falcon.' Another ancient custom of the Eurasian nomads, that of associating a chieftain's horse with his burial, persisted in Asia Minor into the 13th century. Although no known early Seljukid burial contained the body of a horse, when Keykâvus I brought his father's body to Konya for reburial in 1210, he held a feast in memory of the late Sultan and gave instructions that the latter's favourite charger was to attend it.[49]

Sometimes, as in the case of Sarukan's son or of Turumtay, Emir of Amasia, the Seljuks embalmed their dead. Some scholars ascribe this practice to Byzantine influence, but the excavations conducted at Pazirik in the Altai[50] have shown that the Eurasian nomads made use of the process from at any rate as far back as the 5th or 4th centuries B.C. In Asia Minor, the Seljuks laid their dead on their backs, inclining their heads to the right so that when the coffin was set in place in the türbe, facing the door opening towards Mecca, the eyes of the dead were directed towards the holy city.

Among their daily activities the Seljuks derived their greatest HAWKING
pleasure from hunting and hawking. A special official bearing the title of beg or prince was in charge of the royal hunt, and the sovereign expected all his able-bodied courtiers to take part Plate 58
in the day's proceedings; in the evening, he would reward the one with the biggest bag. Malik Shah was so devoted to the sport that he always carried a notebook about with him in which he recorded his personal observations on the day's events. It is impossible not to wonder whether it may not have been this habit of his which gave Frederick II Hohenstaufen the idea for his great book on falconry.

It took many years before the average Seljuk could be per- TENTS AND
suaded to exchange his ancestral tent for a house. These tents PALACES
were of the Central Asian type, that is, they were round and Plate 33
made of interlaced rushes, while their pointed roofs were formed of bent withies; the whole structure was covered with felt panels, which were often ornamented on the outside. Under the impact of Persian influence the Sultan and his courtiers were the first to become attracted by the thought of living in a palace, though, perhaps because 'town was ever a prison to a Turk', their conception of a palace took the form of a number of detached pavilions, which were linked into an architectural

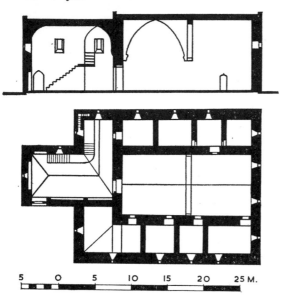

Fig. 5. Elevation and plan of the Haidar Bey Kiosk.

5 0 5 10 15 20 25 M.

Fig. 5

whole by an encircling wall. Like the Ottoman Sultans in the Serai Palace, they had separate buildings or *kiosks* housing the sovereign's private apartments and his harem, there were detached council halls, immense kitchens capable of feeding hundreds of people, pavilions in which the Sultan's clothes and plate were kept, others containing the textiles and robes of honour intended as presents for their guests; possibly even, as in the case of certain other Muslim sovereigns, a *tiraz* or silk-weaving workshop of their own.[51] There were also separate riding schools, detached stables, special quarters for housing the royal hunt, an armoury, food stores and chancelleries, with many little gardens with pools of water and fountains to adorn them.

NEW
BUILDING
Plates 1, 7, 9, 11

In the 12th century the Seljuks' first thought, on capturing a town, was the repair of its fortifications and the provision of a mosque, so that it was not long before the slender minaret

96

came to take its place in a landscape which had until then known only the dome. Then the conically-roofed mausolea began to spring up here and there, altering the skyline still further. At the same time the living conditions in the towns were improved by the creation of such essential institutions as medical and theological colleges, hospitals, mental homes, orphanages and poor-houses.

In the Christian world, for all its learning and culture, administrators had not given much thought to the provision of hospitals for the poor; the Eastern rulers proved more alive to the needs of the people. From the 9th century onwards most of the leading Islamic cities possessed hospitals and charitable institutions of various sorts, and it was as a result of the impact which the Saracenic world made on the Western that a school of medicine was established at Salerno towards the end of that century. Its existence influenced the Benedictine monks of Monte Cassino, leading them to expand their own dispensary, and this in turn resulted, late in the 12th century, in the creation of schools of medicine at the universities of Montpellier, Bologna, Padua and Paris. By this time, however, the Seljuks had transformed their sultanate into a veritable Welfare State, and although the incentive to do so may have come in the first place from Transoxiana and Persia, where some hospitals and medical schools had been established in the 10th century, the wide-scale application of these services was an essentially Seljukid accomplishment.

The view put forward by many 19th-century scholars that the Seljuks brought nothing but chaos and desolation to Asia Minor is not borne out by the facts. Although the Seljuks were involved in warfare almost every year, they yet found time to sponsor the construction of far more hospitals and charitable foundations than they fought battles. In their hands a region which had been sadly lacking in social services became one of

G

the best-provided with them. The transformation was rapidly effected by means of private endowments and bequests, the sovereigns and their families setting the example to their courtiers. Keyhüsrev I was among the first to found a medical school and hospital, doing so at Kayseri in honour of his sister. In this dual foundation the two buildings stood side by side; they were connected by a covered corridor, and were known by the name Şifaiye Medrese.[52] The medical staff attached to the hospital taught both in the school and at the bedsides of the sick, much as is the practice today in the world's foremost teaching hospitals.

The foundation of the Şifaiye Medrese was rapidly followed by that of many more. A similar foundation, the Darul Çifte Medrese or Daruşşifa at Sivas, served the Ottoman Empire as a model of its kind. Its staff included specialists in internal diseases as well as surgeons and oculists, and the medical books in its well-stocked library were available to students as well as to the staff. Some of these Seljukid hospitals remained in use in Turkey until well into the 19th century, others perished earlier; a few even survived until the First World War, if not in the splendid buildings in which the Seljuks had installed them, then in newer ones, for the Ottomans continued to respect the original endowments. Even when it became necessary to re-house an old hospital they endeavoured to preserve its original name, and to keep as close as possible to the terms of its foundation charter.

The Seljuks' fondness for good drinking water and their interest in medicine led them to appreciate and to make use of many of the mineral springs which abound in Anatolia. Kılıçarslan II had particular faith in the waters of Havza and, in 1161, he built two baths there. The baths at Kırşehir, Ilgın, Yoncal and Hamidiye were among the most popular, while certain other springs were reserved for the use of horses and other valuable animals. Over two hundred spas are mentioned in surviving records[53] and the actual number in use was probably much larger. The majority were equipped with sumptuous bathing establishments and drinking fountains.

The creation of a hospital service in which people received free treatment and free board and lodging did not represent the full extent of Seljukid benevolence; money was also found for the establishment of numerous poor-houses, orphanages and mental homes, where the services provided were likewise given free of charge. But the Seljuks devoted even more thought and money to meeting the need for schools and religious seminaries, and consequently their state was exceptionally well provided with educational institutions.

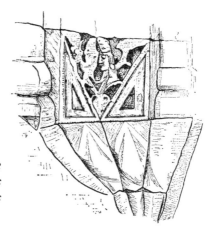

Fig. 6. Sculptured heads from the inside of a pilaster on the portal to Divriği's Mental Hospital, possibly the portraits of its builders.

Though the Seljuks were unable to prevent the decline of agriculture in the areas in which most of the wars were fought, they endeavoured to develop local industries, such as the production of alum and of refined sugar, for they realized that a stable economy was of paramount importance if their state was to survive. In the opening decades of their rule they had relied for their revenue primarily on the tributes which they levied from

REVENUE

their vassals. These payments were partly made in money, partly in kind. Additional income was supplied by the booty captured in battle, which often produced considerable sums. That seized from Leo II of Armenia, for example, was reported to have turned the scales at a hundred and twenty thousand pounds; yet, in addition, the King was forced to supply his conquerors with fifteen hundred trained soldiers a year.

Although the spoils of war provided the exchequer with useful sums till the time of the Mongol invasion, they soon ceased to meet the State's growing expenditure and it became necessary for the Seljuks to seek new sources of income. They found these in trade. When they realized that the commerce in Christian slaves was proving exceedingly profitable they did everything in their power to expand it, setting out to maintain the supply partly by purchase, partly by the kidnapping of young children and also by capturing villagers whose lands they overran in time of war. Georgians fetched especially high prices, selling easily and very profitably. Even so, it soon became apparent that even the slave trade, lucrative though it remained, could not suffice, and it became necessary to encourage and increase the flow of transit goods across Anatolia.

CARAVAN-
SERAIS

As a first step in this direction the government ordered the repair of the old caravan routes which, dating back to deep antiquity, had served generations of Roman and Byzantine merchants. The Byzantines had allowed these roads to deteriorate; the Seljuks now set about repairing them, strengthening the

Plate 23

unsafe bridges and building magnificent new stone ones. Then, for the first time in the long history of these ancient highways, they provided them with a network of rest-houses, the most

Plates 15–22

splendid of which were called *Sultan Hans* or *caravanserais*, while the somewhat less fine were known as *hans*. The majority were superb structures and some were palatial. They were established at convenient intervals along the major trade routes to provide a safe and comfortable resting-place for caravans, at which the men and beasts relaxed for a night to recuperate from the effects of an arduous day of travel. The distance between each of these establishments was calculated on the basis of nine hours' travel by camel, or about 18 miles, the equivalent of a day's journey, so that a caravan making an early start was sure of reaching the han's hospitable roof by nightfall.

As the caravan drew near, the han's defence towers and the massive dressed stone walls would take shape; then, gradually, the intricate interlaced designs and honeycomb niches of the elaborately sculptured doorways would grow more clearly visible. Inside, every comfort was available. At the hans established in the towns an entry and an exit tax were levied, but no charges were made in the roadside caravanserais. Inside the entrance gate the traveller's eyes rested first on the mosque and its ablution fountain, where thanks could be offered to God for the protection vouchsafed that day; then the great bales of goods could be unloaded and stored in the strong-rooms provided for that purpose, and the tired beasts be led to the excellent stables fitted with stone troughs.

Fig. 7. Tercan Han, late 12th century; on the left, entrance to the travellers' quarters; on the right, to the stables.

The men could choose for their sleeping-quarters between private rooms and dormitories. A bath house, coffee and repair shops of various kinds were also to be found. Meals were served, and certain of the larger establishments, notably the Sultan Han on the Konya–Aksaray road and the Karatay Han

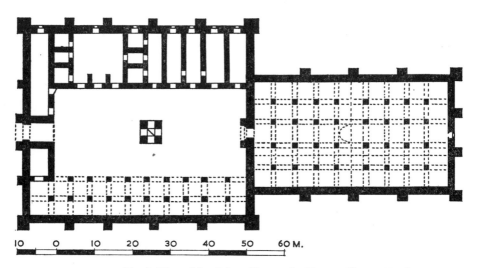

Fig. 8. Plan of the Sultan Han on the Konya–Aksaray Road, 1229.

on the Kayseri–Malatya road, even kept a band of musicians for the delight of their guests. Where there were no musicians, the travellers diverted each other by talking of the wonders they had seen, the dangers they had surmounted and the strange and interesting things they had heard on their journeys. In the towns, people flocked to the great vaulted halls of the hans to listen to the astute merchants, the learned scholars and the holy pilgrims, whose conversation was of so high a quality that it transformed a mere rest-house into a 'university for the poor'.

Security on the road was all-important if trade was to flourish. To ensure it, hans situated in the more dangerous districts were supplied with a garrison and a stock of arms. In the 13th century users of the dangerous road to Erzurum had to pay a special tax, levied on each beast of burden, and the money thus collected was spent on policing the road.[54]

The bulk of the trade was of a transit character. At first most of it was centred on Konya, Sivas and Kayseri, where it was handled by the Greek and Armenian carpet merchants, for in the 12th century the Seljuks were only interested in controlling the horse and cattle trade. A hundred years later, however, the Italians discovered that large profits were to be derived from the transit trade and the Venetian *podesta* in Constantinople lost no time in asking Giyaseddin Keyhüsrev I for commercial privileges for his countrymen. The Sultan was anxious to see commerce expand and he did not object to the presence of Venetians in his realm. His views were shared by his son and successor, Izzeddin Keykâvus I, and both rulers were soon so well satisfied with the results of the first, somewhat tentative concessions to which they had agreed that, in 1220, the Podesta Jacopo Tiepolo was able to sign a comprehensive trade agreement with Keykûbad I.[55] By the terms of this treaty the Venetians acquired the right to carry precious stones, pearls, gold and silver ingots as well as money and corn free of duty, although a tax of 2·5 per cent was levied on all other goods. Mutual measures of security were agreed upon, and provision was made for the loss of goods at sea; finally, procedure was established for punishing the unruly, it being decided that quarrels between Venetians and other Latins, such as the Pisans or the men from Provence, should be dealt with by a Venetian tribunal, whilst brawls involving the Seljuks and Franks, and cases of murder or theft would be brought before a Seljukid court.

The Latin conquest of Constantinople led to an increase in the number of Western merchants setting out to seek their fortune in the Levant, and as a result a good deal of the trade which had until then been transacted by the Greeks passed into the hands of the Venetians. The volume of traffic had by now greatly increased and was no longer limited to transit goods, for the Seljuks had developed a considerable import and export trade of their own. Much of this commerce centred on Sivas where most of the Seljukid merchants had settled, acting as both buyers and sellers, and also as forwarding agents, since traders from Syria and Iraq, and more particularly from Mosul, had formed the habit of bringing their goods to Sivas and handing them over there to a Seljukid representative. The latter then became responsible for assembling a caravan destined for Sinop or Trebizond, whence the goods were forwarded by sea to ports on the eastern and southern coasts of the Black Sea.

The Trapezuntine trade was especially important, to no small degree because of the regular links which it maintained with its vassal city of Perateia (Cherson).[56] In Sivas a tax was levied on all goods carried to the coast, and although the Greek Emperor of Trebizond received a share of the profit from the goods which crossed his empire, it was the Seljuks who controlled the port of Sinop, and who carried on a particularly lively trade with the Kipchaks of southern Russia and the Russian and Tartar traders using the Crimean port of Sudak, or Soldaia. Sudak served as the meeting-place for all Turkish merchants travelling to or from Russia, carrying 'ermines and grey furres with other rich and costly skins, as well as with cotton cloth, cobalt, silks and spices.'[57]

Sometimes a Syrian or Iraki merchant preferred to accompany his goods to their final destination instead of entrusting them to an agent. In such cases the trader would travel to Sinop, embarking thence for Sudak with his bales of silks and cottons, and his consignments of spices. The fact that he chartered his own vessel and travelled with his goods did not exempt him from the obligation to return to Sinop with a ship-load of slaves and furs, for the Sultan looked upon these goods as his most valuable imports.[58] Indeed, Keykûbad I's daring attack on Sudak in 1222 may well have been provoked by some damage to one such consignment or expedition.

Although Sinop proved an immense asset to Seljukid trade, in the 13th century it was the inland town of Sivas which, rather surprisingly, was of an importance comparable to that of the major commercial cities of the Levant. Its significance was still so great in the 14th century that the Florentine diplomat Baldone thought it desirable to include in the commercial guide *La Practica Della Mercature,* which he had compiled for the use of Italian merchants, a comparative table of the weights and measures in use in Sivas, Lajazzo, Cyprus and Acre. The Mongol occupation of Rum did not impede the trade, which remained so flourishing that, in 1276, the Genoese decided to open a consulate at Sivas and to enter into diplomatic relations with the Mongols.

By the second quarter of the 13th century the Seljuks had become to some extent an exporting nation, but their imports still greatly outnumbered the goods they sent abroad. A list of these imports serves to throw some light on the standard of living enjoyed by the Seljuks. The goods most in demand from Egypt were spices, sugar, arms and cotton, though Hama and Aleppo provided the finest cotton, while a certain amount of very inferior quality came from Little Armenia. Baghdad supplied the very fine, light-weight wool which was used exclusively for the turbans worn by the Sultan and his ministers of state, as well as some of the delicate silks which were reserved for their robes. Consignments of musk, aloes and ambergris accompanied these wares. Silks of even finer quality and greater value were brought from China, and the supply of home-produced carpets was supplemented by imports from Persia, and more especially from Shiraz, as well as from Transoxiana. Many of the precious stones of which the Sultan and his courtiers were so fond came from Central Asia, while Georgia helped to maintain the supply of thoroughbred horses. Russia produced unlimited quantities of furs, and the slave markets throughout the sultanate were constantly kept filled with the Caucasian men and women whom the Turks prized above all others as personal servants.

SHIPPING The Provençales who controlled the Cypriot trade and the Genoese who had taken over that of Egypt handled the shipping even when the Seljuks had become masters of Antalya. Its capture in 1207 had been a major triumph for the Seljuks. Within a short time such wealth had poured into their coffers from its port dues that the Sultan determined to acquire another outlet on the same seaboard. However, it fell to his brother Keykûbad to achieve this in 1220 by the capture of Candelore or Scandelore, as it was called, where the harbour facilities were even better than at Antalya. Renaming it Alaiye after himself, the Sultan set about transforming the port into a

Fig. 9 naval base by adding an arsenal and secret dock to the existing facilities. These alterations did not interfere with Alaiye's role as a commercial centre;[59] rather they helped to expand it. The increased flow of its trade drew a mixed population of Saracens, Greeks and Jews to the town; each of these communities established itself in a separate quarter, and they were speedily joined by an influx of Latin merchants who proceeded to install themselves in yet another district, whence they traded in cloth brought from Challon, Narbonne and Perpignan, as well as in silks made in Lombardy and gold embroidery-thread and fine camelots imported from Cyprus. The Florentines formed the largest section of the European community. But all, regardless of nationality, were obliged to pay the Seljuks a 2 per cent tax on all the goods they handled. They could well afford to do so for the Mediterranean shipping route had become so safe that their losses at sea were well-nigh negligible.

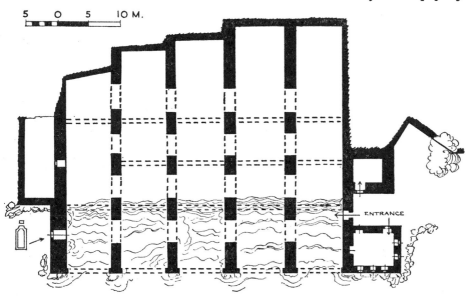

Fig. 9. The Tersane or dockyard, Alaiye, 1228.

In contrast to the Mediterranean, the waters of the Black Sea   PIRACY
were infested with pirates. By the latter half of the 13th century
the Sinop route was fraught with danger. The port had become
the hereditary fief of the sons of the Pervane Muin ed din, and
that statesman's wild relatives used it as a base for their preda-
tory raids on merchant shipping. In 1279 no less a person than
the Pervane's nephew was seized by the crews of two Genoese
vessels and carried off to Italy in punishment for his piratical
activities. He was held a captive there till the payment of a huge
ransom secured his release. In 1313 a certain Gazi Celebi,
ruler of Sinop and Kastamonu, who was either a descendent
of the Pervane or possibly even a son of Sultan Mesud II,[60]
contrived to sink several Genoese ships anchored at Sinop by
diving beneath them and holing their hulls.[61]

MARKETS Well-organized markets were yet another of the amenities which the Seljuks provided with a view to encouraging trade. They were to be found in all the major cities, and in each the specific trades were grouped together in separate parts of the bazaar. Even secondary cities such as Erzincan were equipped with markets of such size and splendour that they aroused the admiration of as seasoned a traveller as Ibn Batuta. It is scarcely surprising then that the Sultan and all those connected with the court and with commerce grew so rich that they could afford to build and endow the edifices on which their fame still rests, and at the same time to satisfy their taste for luxuries. In some sections of society there was such an abundance of wealth that Keyhüsrev II had no hesitation in paying a hundred and eighty thousand dirrhems for a single ruby, and in 1224, the Genoese merchant Simon Lercani found it necessary to take six hundred dirrhems with him when travelling from Alaiye to Sivas.[62]

TAXATION Most of the population was subjected to taxation. Town-dwellers paid their dues to the civil administrators, the holders of military fiefs to their superior officers, those living on land belonging to the Wakf or religious authority paid theirs to the representatives of that body, and private property owners sent their payments to the treasury; taxes were also levied on flocks and on the grain harvest as well as on unmarried men; but religious foundations of all denominations were exempted.

THE PEASANTRY Unfortunately, however, prosperity was by no means universal. The greatest poverty was to be found in the outlying districts, where many of the peasants spent their lives in conditions of extreme squalor. This was not due to any fault of their own; proof sufficient of the efficiency of their husbandry was to be seen in the belt of market gardens which encircled Konya, stretching far out into the barren Anatolian plain. The dire

want in which so many of them lived was due to the destruc⁄
tion of their crops and irrigation trenches by the armies which
almost every year traversed their laboriously⁄cultivated fields.
Even the Byzantines had found that although pastoral activities
could to some extent be maintained in the vicinity of battle⁄
fields, it was impossible to cultivate the land and raise good
crops in the regions through which the armies passed. In Asia
Minor the standard of living had in fact sharply declined among
the agriculturists for some years prior to the Seljukid conquest
of the region.

In the 13th century the poverty⁄stricken Anatolian peasantry
proved a ready prey to the numerous mendicant preachers who
fled into Asia Minor in face of the Mongol advance. Dervishes
from Horasan came spreading the Ismaili creed; they were fol⁄
lowed by begging pilgrims from as far away as Ardebil,
Baghdad and Syria, fostering the latent discontent; holy men
from Central Asia aggravated unrest by inciting the peasants to
forsake their land to seek an easier livelihood in safer districts
further to the west. In 1239/40 a Syrian dervish from Urfa
called by some Baba Işak, by other Baba Eliys, installed himself
in a cave overlooking Amasya and presented himself as a
prophet. His sham piety won him a large following of Turco⁄
mans who, encouraged by the dervish, called upon the people
of Malatya to rise in revolt and march westward. The revolt
spread rapidly, embracing Sivas, Tokat and Aksaray, so that
it became necessary for Keyhüsrev II to send troops to deal with
the rebels; but it was only when reinforcements had been
brought from as far afield as Erzurum that order was restored
and the dervish leader captured. Baba Işak and his lieutenants
were harshly dealt with; they were put to death in 1241 by
burning and hanging, whilst their supporters had their property
confiscated, and had silently to look on while it was being
divided between the troops and the charitable foundations
specified by the Sultan.

The dirrhem of Iconium served as the official currency. It was generally struck with the reigning Sultan's name, though some of the royal claimants to the throne contrived to mint coins bearing their own names. The very large numbers of Seljukid coins which appear in the hoards still being unearthed as far afield as Transcaucasia serve to indicate how widely they were used. The earliest coins were struck by Seljuk's grandsons at Nishapur and Merv, with designs derived from Abbasid prototypes. Later the Great Seljuks added a touch of ornamentation to their designs, showing a preference for arabesque motifs, but the rulers of Rum proved more daring. Though the majority preferred to restrict themselves to the use of script, several sultans introduced some representational shapes. Thus, Ruknûddin Süleyman Shah, perhaps influenced by Kwarazmian, Sasanian or even Byzantine examples, stamped the face of his coins with the figure of a horseman holding a sword to his shoulder and with a star set on either side of his haloed head.

Keyhüsrev II may have had other reasons besides the wish to honour his wife when he chose to stamp his coins with representations of the sun coupled with the figure of a lion.[63] Both these devices were ancient symbols of sovereignty; Firdausi, in his preface to the *Shahnamah*, compared a king who was about to give battle to 'a lion with the face of the sun'. The crescent also appeared on many Seljukid coins, notably on those of Keyhüsrev II. The majority of the coins were minted at Konya, Sivas and Erzincan, but there were short periods when minor princes issued coins in such towns as Ankara, Baiburt or Erzurum. Their quality varied greatly, the best copper coins belonging in the main to the reign of Ruknûddin Süleyman Shah and the best silver ones to Kılıçarslan II. Alaeddin Keykûbad I was the first to mint gold coins, but by that time the currency issued by the Caliph of Baghdad, by the Fatimids, and by the Begs of Aleppo, as well as the Italian florin, were all accepted as legal tender throughout the sultanate.

It is difficult, indeed well-nigh impossible, to form any very exact idea of the size of the Seljukid population of Asia Minor in the 12th and 13th centuries, for the only census that was ever taken there was organized by the Mongols to enable them to introduce a universal system of taxation, and by that time conditions throughout the empire had altered so greatly that the figure can throw little light on the size of the population at the time of the kingdom's greatness. In Persia, Malık Shah had an army of 400,000 men when he came to the throne, but he reduced it to a force of about 70,000;[64] the Sultans of Rum were likewise able to assemble vast armies, but it has not so far been proved possible to establish the proportion of Ghuzz, Turcoman or other mercenaries enrolled in them; nor can the exact date be ascertained at which tribute in the form of trained soldiers was first levied by the sultans.

By the 13th century a population of 100,000 is ascribed to such cities as Konya, Sivas and Kayseri, but here again the figure is not of any real use since there is no means of discovering the number of the Greeks and Armenians who had refused to abandon their old homes at the time of the Seljukid conquest, nor that of the Jews and Saracens who found employment in these towns when prosperity returned to them. The craftsmen's guilds contained men of many diverse nationalities and creeds, all of whom had, however, to submit to Muslim authority. On the face of it, it appears unlikely that the Seljuks can have constituted a majority; their difficulty in controlling the nomads seems to confirm this assumption, and we should therefore think of them as filling the officer and administrative grades and exerting control of affairs through these channels rather than by the weight of their numbers.

The Seljukid authorities, concerned though they were with the material and physical welfare of the people, were not blind to the importance of their spiritual well-being. The ardour with

Figs. 10, 11

which the Seljuks had first embraced Islam was maintained throughout the centuries following their conversion by the fervour with which each successive generation fulfilled its self-appointed duty of safeguarding the legitimate Caliph and of defending the orthodox creed. This outlook led the Seljuks to view the construction of splendid mosques and great theological colleges as a task of outstanding worth. Humility was a virtue to which even the Sultans strove to attain. The inscription on the outer door of the mausoleum of Keykâvus I at Sivas expresses this attitude. 'Here below', it reads, 'are many sovereigns who from the peak of their might reached the Pleiades with their arrows and grazed the Heavenly Twins with the tips of their lances. See now, as with the daughters of the Great Bear, how the hand of death has smashed their lances and broken their arrows.'

The establishment at Konya of the headquarters of the Mevlevi Order of Dervishes helped to maintain the deep

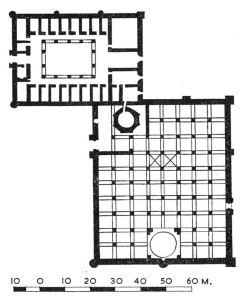

10 0 10 20 30 40 50 60 M.

Fig. 10. Plan of the mosque, mausoleum and medrese which, with a bath of which all traces have now disappeared, formed the Mahperi Huand Foundation, Kayseri, 1237/38.

Fig. 11. Marble lintel from the outer wall of the Alaeddin Mosque, Ko..ya, 1219/20.

devoutness of the religious outlook in the face of the agnosticism provoked by the Mongols; and the use of the native Turkish tongue in preference to the literary languages of Persia and Arabia for the great mystical works that were written at the time helped to strengthen belief in the Muslim faith, without leading to any fanatical outbursts against the Christians and Jews. Jewish doctors as well as Greek and Armenian scholars continued to be made as welcome at court as were the sages and poets of Islam. Something of the chivalrous spirit of Saladin and the intellectual curiosity of Frederick II Hohenstaufen en-nobled the outlook of the Seljukid rulers. Though unimagina-tive by temperament and somewhat puritanical in their views, they responded to visual beauty and to distinction of mind. They were ready to be charmed by new forms and ideas, and they were inclined to take up and toy for a while with alien ways, without necessarily pausing to consider whether the latter conflicted with the basic tenets of their own faith.

The infiltration of foreign ideas may well have been brought about by the Greeks and Armenians who, on the Seljuks' rise

H

to power, embraced Islam in order to preserve their property, but who nevertheless continued to cling to certain Christian habits, doing so with such fervour that these eventually became incorporated into the Seljukid tradition. With the Christian state of Little Armenia to the east of the sultanate, with Greeks and Crusaders on its western boundaries, and with numerous Christians living within the realm, it would indeed have been surprising had the Seljuks escaped all trace of Christian in-fluence.

At some times the Christian element became particularly marked; in the latter half of the 13th century it was sufficiently strong to induce the Patriarch Anthemius to think that Key-kâvus II had secretly become a Christian, and that other con-verts were to be found among members of the Ismaili and Bektaşi sects. In Aleppo, Nüreddin Sengi, a man revered for his piety, often expressed misgivings concerning the orthodoxy of the Seljuks of Asia Minor, and other Muslim divines shared his doubts. The charge of showing excessive partiality towards Christians was repeatedly levelled at the later sultans. On one occasion the Chief Cadi even dared to accuse Giyaseddin Keyhüsrev to his face of the sins of free thinking and of having an exaggerated admiration for the Byzantine way of life; in his anger the affronted Sultan struck and inadvertently killed his minister. When a drought followed the Cadi's death and people began to regard it as a sign of divine anger the Sultan repented of his loss of temper, yet he would not publicly abjure the deed. But variegated though the society of Konya may at times have been, its outlook remained to the end fundamentally and essentially Turkish, and its attitude and reactions to life fer-vently Islamic; in this it was always fully in accord with the spirit of the people.

CHAPTER IV

Religious and Secular Thought and Literature

> He dieth not who giveth life to learning.
>
> A saying of Muhammad.

ARABIAN INTELLECTUALS had become fascinated by the works of the great thinkers of India and ancient Greece at quite an early date in their history. Under the influence of these early philosophers two schools of thought grew up in Arabia, the one more active, the other more contemplative. The members of the former, the more forthright of the two, were known as the Walkers; they did not exercise much influence on the development of Seljukid culture. The second group, the Contemplatives, was, however, to play a considerable part in moulding the Turkish outlook, for many of the metaphysical and mystical scholars who were to produce the major philosophical and literary works of the Seljukid period adopted the views of these thinkers. The influence of the Contemplatives became particularly marked in the 10th century, under the Abbasids, when the discovery of the works of Aristotle, whose subtle reasoning appealed irresistibly to the nimble-minded Arabs, stimulated a form of religious disputation known as the *Kalam*. The arguments put forward in the Kalam were expected to conform to the Aristotelian pattern, that is to say to be intellectual in conception and dialectical in form, but this, naturally enough, rendered them unacceptable to the mystics, who wished to see a more spiritual doctrine approached in a more emotional manner.

In their search for an ascetic principle the mystics came in touch with a woman whose teaching seemed to express the very sentiments which formed their own outlook. She preached that God was love and she encouraged her numerous followers to develop a dreamy form of spirituality which they found so exhilarating that they delighted in displaying their allegiance to her by wearing a distinctive woollen robe known as the *suf*; as a result those who appeared clothed in it quickly became known as *Sufis* and, before long, the adoption of the robe linked the wearers into a brotherhood that was soon to assume virtually the character of a sect.

Firdausi's *Shahnamah* is permeated with the mysticism which is so much a part of the Sufic outlook; this is not reflected to any great degree in the stories which form the body of the work, but it pervades the numerous maxims and moral and ethical pro-nouncements that are scattered throughout the text. These aphorisms build up into a definite philosophic doctrine and ethical code, for each saying sets out to affirm belief in God's universality, asserting that his essence is diffused throughout the visible and invisible worlds, the union with which the human soul is constantly called upon to strive to attain because it is only when such fusion has been achieved that the soul can at last enjoy permanent tranquillity. In the *Shahnamah* this belief is most clearly reflected in the chapters devoted to the great Sultan Kai Khusraw who, at the height of his fame and power, turned in disgust from the vanities of terrestrial splendour to disappear for ever into the world beyond. Indeed, it may well have been this story, which never failed deeply to move a Muslim audience, that decided Kılıçarslan II to abdicate in favour of his sons.

NORTHERN LITERARY CENTRES

If philosophic thought drew much of its vitality from Baghdad, literature and learning, that is to say mathematics, medicine, geography and history, developed at this time primarily in Central Asia, Transoxiana and Horasan, all of which formed a single cultural unit. While Buhara served as the capital of the Samanids it ranked with the foremost centres of learning in the Orient; this may perhaps have come about partly because the caravan routes linking the Eastern world to the Western met there, bringing to the city the learning both of China and of the classical world, thus stimulating creative thought. The imperial Samanid library was so rich in books that even Avicenna (980–1037) was able to find in it all the works he needed for his own researches; yet within a short time Kiwa, the capital of the Shahs of Kwarazm, became an equally useful and attractive centre for scholars, and soon after, both Balk and Merv developed into towns with a scarcely less flourishing intellectual life of their own.

It is indeed astonishing to see how much talent and learning was to be found in these remote towns in the 10th and 11th centuries, and to note the high proportion of men of Central-Asian origin among those who were largely responsible for the great Persian literary renaissance. Merv, which was renowned for its beauty, seemed to act as a magnet for writers and scholars of all kinds, and it was there that the poet Abu 'l Hasan Shahid, a native of Balk, produced the first *divan*, or collection of lyrics, which was soon to become a characteristic literary form in Persia.

The princes of the house of Saman were nurtured on a tradi-tion of patronage. Nuh II was as keen as his forebears to en-courage the arts and it was he who first thought of commission-ing a Persian version of the Pahlevi *Book of Kings*. He entrusted the task to his court poet, but before that unfortunate man had had time to make much progress with the translation his royal patron developed a dislike of him and had him put to death.

The Sultan did not long outlive the poet, for he and his entire house were soon after themselves destroyed by the founder of the house of Ghazna. Though the new conqueror had to devote most of his time to political and administrative affairs, he too became interested in the task which the last Samanid ruler had set his court poet. The Ghuzz usurper often talked of reviving the project, but it fell to his successor Mahmud (997–1036) to carry it to splendid fruition by engaging the foremost Persian poet of his day, the incomparable Firdausi, yet another native of Tus, to produce the magnificent version of the epic which was to outshine the glories of the Pahlevi original. Under the title of *Shahnamah*, it became the most widely read book in Persia; its effect on the Seljuks of Asia Minor was particularly marked, for it developed in them a liking for and an understanding of history, it provided them with a standard by which to assess their own conduct, and it stimulated their innate sense of nationhood. The entire dynasty of Rum loved the book and found in it inspiration for their choice of titles; some of them even arranged for quotations from its text to be inscribed upon the walls of Konya and Sivas, where all might read and reflect upon their meaning.

Firdausi spent thirty-five years at the Ghaznavid court but, on leaving it, he considered himself so poorly rewarded for his service that he wrote a pungent satire on his tyrannical patron— a satire which, whatever the rights or wrongs of the case, succeeded in damning Mahmud not only in the eyes of his contemporaries but also in those of later generations. In the 12th century the scientist Anwari of Tus revenged himself on Sultan Sencer for a display of meanness by following Firdausi's example and writing a mordant poem about his royal master. The verses were handed round and had an immense success; eventually they came into the hands of the poet Suzani, who was living in Samarkand. Suzani was so enchanted by them that he decided to try his hand at writing comic verses; he too succeeded so well in this vein that his attempt inspired a whole group of poets living in northern Persia and Transoxiana. Among the less 'broad' of these poems the best works took the form of parodies or humorous moralities. Eventually these culminated in distant Anatolia in a national Turkish style, the most famous example of which—the collection of *Tales of the Nazareddin Hodja*—are still as popular in Turkey today as when Mrs Ewing published the less ribald of them for the delight of the children of Victorian England.

The intellectual activity which was taken so much for granted at the Samanid, Ghaznavid and Kwarazmian courts must have made a strong impression on the Seljuks from the moment when they settled on the lower reaches of the Oxus and entered into regular relations with these cultivated rulers. Nor is it reasonable to suppose that all the Seljuks were illiterate at the time. Even if Alp Arslan, and as is suggested, Sencer also, were unable to read—which seems unlikely—there is evidence of the existence from quite an early date of a class of educated Seljuks. A written form of Turkish had been in use in Central Asia from as early as the 6th century and may have evolved well before; at any rate by this date certain of the Ghuzz already possessed a class of scribes who were proficient in the use of their native language. When necessary, the Orkhon Ilk-Khagan or supreme ruler, and even some of his Khakans or tribal chieftains, could call upon a scribe who had a fair knowledge of written Persian and Arabic, or a smattering of them, as well as his own tongue, though the number of these qualified men must have varied considerably both with the period and the tribe.

The earliest examples of written Turkish known to us are a series of funerary inscriptions, many of them of a political character, relating to the Kül Tepe or Bilge Khan dynasties who reigned in the Orkhon valley in Mongolia from about the 6th to the 8th century A.D. Though the inscriptions were discovered in the 18th century they were not deciphered until a hundred years later, when Professor Vilhelm Thomsen of Copenhagen associated certain of the letters which appeared in them with some Aramaic ones, and then discovered that the Orkhon alphabet was to some extent a variant of the Soghdian

THE
ORKHON
INSCRIP-
TIONS

or East Persian as it appeared at the beginning of the present era, when the Buhara-Samarkand region constituted the kingdom of Soghd. Thomsen also found that the Turkish used in these inscriptions was already based on the principle of sound harmony which governs the language today. There is reason to think that in their early days the Seljuks remembered and continued to chant a number of epics and songs which had been popular among their forebears,[65] though with their conversion to Islam and their penetration into Persia they abandoned the bulk of this native literary culture. It was at about this time that they adopted the Arabic script, using it thenceforth for their state documents and their official correspondence, as well as for their religious books and the inscriptions which they favoured for the façades of their buildings. Nevertheless, it was the culture and literature of Persia which generally influenced their way of life, their thought and taste, and much of their literary output.

THE NIZAM AL MULK

In the 11th century the Seljukid outlook was shaped primarily by the Nizam al Mulk. The Vizir was both a great statesman and a gifted writer. He was born in Tus in 1019 and was forty-two years old when Alp Arslan raised him to the vizirship. His preference for the Persian language did much to further its use in official correspondence; the Nizam used it when communicating with the Seljuks of Rum and also when writing his own books. The most important of his works is the treatise on government which he compiled for the help of his pupil, the future Malık Shah. In it he mingled practical advice with profound observations on the nature of government.

Not content with being himself a writer, the Nizam set out to attract authors of distinction to his sovereign's court. Foremost among these was Omar Khayyam, a man chiefly renowned in the West as a poet whose lovely quatrains, in FitzGerald's inspired translations, gained world-wide renown. Yet among his contemporaries these verses were regarded as little more than the delightful frivolities with which a convivial man of genius diverts his friends. In an age when great store was set on mathematics, not least because they served as an introduction to the study of the occult, he ranked with the foremost mathematicians of his age. It was in this capacity that the Nizam attached him to Alp Arslan's court, where he provided Khayyam with an up-to-date observatory. The calculations and observations which the poet made there enabled him to reform the existing calendar; his version was brought into use with the Persian New Year of 1079, and it continues to be known in present times as the Celalian or Seljukid calendar.

The Nizam looked far beyond the confines of his sovereign's palace, trying to spread learning throughout the empire by inducing suitable people to devote themselves to the study of law and theology. He appealed to them to do so in many of his public pronouncements, tried to attract them by raising the salaries of teachers, and endeavoured to draw the most distinguished men of the day into the teaching profession by founding libraries for their use, as well as by heaping honours upon them. Then, in his anxiety to expand the study of science, he set about reorganizing the educational establishments, transforming many of the religious seminaries, which had until then been the only dispensers of learning throughout the empire, into state schools in which a wide range of subjects was taught. Furthermore, he insisted that the teachers employed in these institutions should be paid according to a fixed scale and that needy pupils should be helped by means of state grants. Finally he endowed Baghdad with its university. It was called the Nizamiye after him, and the Vizir persuaded the greatest scholars of the Islamic world, including the learned and saintly Abu Hamid Muhammad al Ghazali, to teach in it. Though the idea of a *medrese* or university may have originated in India, where the Buddhists had for long possessed theological schools of university status, the Nizam was probably influenced by the example of Transoxiana or Horasan, where similar institutions had existed on a smaller scale since the 10th century.

However, al Ghazali was not so much interested in teaching as he was anxious to put an end to the practice of the Kalam, which had again become extremely popular among the theo/logical and intellectual circles of Baghdad. He disapproved of the practice because he felt convinced that reason alone could never disclose the ultimate truth, that only absolute faith and implicit belief in God could do so. His teaching thus came very close to that of the Mystics, and it was not long before this very sincere and devout man felt obliged to give up his chair of theology at the Nizamiye University in order to adopt an ascetic way of life, that he might, as he himself put it, 'practice religion as well as preach it'. Many of his former pupils and members of his congregation followed his example to the extent of becoming Sufis, thereby greatly adding to the impor/tance of that movement.

CELALED/
DIN AL
RUMI

Sufi'ism did not, however, find its spiritual home in Baghdad, nor even in Persia, whence it drew many of its most prominent divines. It was in Konya, under the guidance of the greatest Sufi of all, the Mawla Celaleddin al Rumi, the founder of the Mawlana or Mevlevi Order of the Dancing or Spinning Dervishes, that its philosophy was finally crystallized and its literature brought to its highest level. Celaleddin was of Persian origin; he was born at Balk in the year 1207. His father, Bahaeddin Veled, came of a rich and noble house, tracing his descent back to the Caliph Abu Bakr and to Alaeddin ibn Tukuş, Shah of Kwarazm (1190–1220), through the latter's daughter Malika ibn Jahan. The connection would have en/titled Bahaeddin to a place at court, but the love of indepen/dence characteristic of the north/eastern Persian of this date was so strongly developed in the young man that he preferred to study medicine and to establish himself as a doctor in his native city. There his skill quickly made him famous and his innate kindliness won him the love of the people. His renown spread beyond the walls of Balk and, inevitably, before long it had reached court circles, and aroused the jealousy and animosity of the powerful. By 1212 the doctor's position had become so dangerous that he decided to flee his native land. Taking his family with him, he sought refuge first in Malatya and then in Erzincan. His reputation had preceded him, and in Rum he was made welcome wherever he went, none pausing to consider whether this display of warmth would be likely to annoy the powerful ruler of Kwarazm or anger the Caliph and his divines, many of whom disapproved of the doctor's religious views. In fact Bahaeddin was overwhelmed with both public and private offers of hospitality, and within only a few months of his arrival he was appointed principal of Laranda (Karaman) University.

It was at about the time at which Bahaeddin took up his duties at Laranda that his young son Celaleddin became subject to ecstasies and visions. The boy's intellectual gifts were already outstanding and his sensitivity was so exceptional that his father decided to take personal charge of his education. The family had not spent many years at Laranda before reports of the remarkable talent of both father and son reached the Sultan and his court at Konya. Alaeddin Keykûbad I lost little time in inviting the household to settle in the capital. There the young Celaleddin became generally admired for his goodness and learning. His marriage in 1226 to Çanhar Hatun, the daughter of Lala Sharafeddin of Samarkand—a choice which served to strengthen the family's links with Central Asia—gave wide satisfaction.

Bahaeddin Veled died in Konya in 1231 and his death left Celaleddin unhappy and unsettled. To ease his depression the young man set out for Aleppo and Damascus in order to pursue his studies in the sciences at these great seats of learning. Yet however much he concentrated on his work it failed to allay his restlessness. An intense longing for spiritual enlightenment took possession of him. He returned to Konya, where he was instantly appointed professor in as many as four different institutions, at the same time becoming an assiduous pupil of one of his father's disciples, the Seyit Burhanuddin Husain of Tidmuth. He spent two years in this way, studying philosophy and theology on conventional lines. Then one day a wandering Sufi, Şemseddin Mehmed of Tabriz, happened to come to Konya. He seemed a wild fellow and little different from the many other indigent dervishes who passed through the town, begging their way from door to door in the manner that had earned them their name of *dervish* or doorstep. Nevertheless, Şemseddin bewitched Celaleddin, who instantly lavished upon him all the deep affection he had formerly devoted to his father. Not content with taking the wandering friar to his heart and home, Celaleddin also embraced the stranger's philosophic doctrine, and eventually even adopted the latter's *talkallus* or signature for his own *ghazals* and mystical verses.

Most of the people of Konya had not been attracted by the itinerant Sufi, and their indifference turned to dislike when his arrogance increased with his feeling of security in Celaleddin's affection. But Celaleddin disregarded the views of his fellow-townsmen, spending his days with Shemseddin, who likewise made no attempt to mend his ways or to win the affection of the people. Eventually dislike of the Sufi grew so strong that it led to rioting in the capital. In the course of the disturbance Şemseddin disappeared, doubtless put to death by the angry mob. His body was never recovered and the mausoleum erected in his name at Konya is a memorial rather than a tomb. Even worse had occurred in the rioting, for Celaleddin's favourite son had been killed while loyally defending his father's cherished guest from the violence of the crowd.

The death of the two people he held most dear plunged
Celaleddin into deep melancholy, and it was during this
period of heart-searching and prayer that inspiration led him
to found the order of the Mevlevi dervishes in memory of his
beloved dead. The costume he devised for the brotherhood was
intended to symbolize mourning. It consisted of a tall white
felt cap, wide sleeveless tunic, a waistband, a jacket and a cloak.

The new Order was open to all men whose behaviour was
good, who were able to accomplish the probationary period of
a thousand and one continuous nights of service, and who were
prepared to devote the remainder of their lives to sincerely
striving to attain to the union of their souls with that of Allah.
This was to be achieved by means of a mystic dance, performed
to special music produced by an orchestra made up of five
instruments: reed flutes, zithers, tambourines, drums and re-
becks.

Because the introduction of music into a religious ceremony
is contrary to Muslim practice, Celaleddin's use of it has
sometimes been ascribed to Christian influence, and indeed, it
may well be that the impact of a piece of music heard in his
childhood, perhaps during some procession connected with the
Greek Orthodox or Latin ritual celebration, made a lasting
impression on his subconscious mind. There is, however,
nothing at all Christian or even specifically Western about the
tune which Celaleddin evolved, which is so essentially Turkish in its rhythm, and of such uncanny and compelling fascina-
tion that it never occurred to any Muslim to take exception to it.

The dance itself exercised a similar spell on both those
who watched it and those taking part. It was based on a
circling movement representing the course of the spheres and
expressing the emotions of a Sufi when his soul overflows with
love for the Almighty. The ecstatic state which enabled the
soul to enter the celestial sphere was attained by means of a rapid
spinning of the body, the dancer gyrating on his left heel with

his arms extended and his head thrown back, yet not breaking the circle or losing his place in the constantly revolving ring of dancers. Each dervish, as he kept time to the curious, rhythmical music, spinning faster and faster, chanted such devout phrases as 'There is no God but God', 'Oh God', 'Oh Him', 'Oh Just God', 'Oh Living God', 'Oh Revengeful God', and so on, till he had reached a state of complete ecstasy and attained elevation.

The Mevlevi were thought to have acquired spiritual powers through their ability to levitate, and it may have been because of this belief that they refused to recognize any authority over themselves other than that of Allah and the master of their Order. The Sultan did not object to this, and he presented Celaleddin with a piece of land in Konya on which to build his monastery. Many wealthy men from Anatolia, some of them married men, hastened to join the new Order and soon additional cloisters were established throughout Asia Minor, on building land granted by the *Wakf* or Religious Authority.

Celaleddin was regarded as a saint during his lifetime and posterity has confirmed this view. With the single exception of his favourite disciple Hüsameddin Çelebi, who became his immediate successor to the directorship of the Order, the leadership of the fraternity remained for all time with Celaleddin's descendants, reverting on Hüsameddin's death to the founder's only surviving son Walad (died 1312). The respect commanded by the latter was so great that he is still generally called Sultan Walad. His talents justified the courtesy, for he was both an able administrator and an outstanding writer; his mystical *mesnevi*, the *Rababnama*, became almost as highly esteemed as his father's monumental work. He was also admired for the delightful verses which he wrote in vernacular Greek, using Arabic letters for the purpose.

At Walad's death the leadership of the Order passed to his heirs, and remained with them till the dissolution of the

Mevlevi, with all the other dervish fraternities, by order of Gazi Mustapha Kemal in 1925. Then the building in Konya which had served them as a mother-house passed, together with the tombs of the Mawlana leaders, into the hands of the Turkish Museum Authorities.

Apart from his collection of lyrics, most of Celaleddin's major works—taking the form either of lectures, letters or maxims presenting a blend of religious and philosophic thought expressed in poetic form—were produced for the Mevlevi dervishes; the idea for the greatest of these compositions—the *Mathnawi-i-ma'nawi* or *Spiritual Mesnevi*—was suggested to him by his disciple Hüsameddin, to whom Celaleddin dictated the whole immense composition, completed on the eve of his death on 17th December 1273. Following to some extent the traditional pattern for works of a religious and moral character, its text of over forty thousand verses in the form of couplets is augmented by the inclusion of commentaries on the Koran and quotations from the Sayings of the Prophet, and the whole is enlivened by the addition of many pleasantries and anecdotes. The poem enjoyed an immediate success, taking its place with the foremost Sufic devotional writings. A thorough familiarity with its text was expected to assure for the reader his everlasting felicity.

After the Mongol invasion Celaleddin began to write in Turkish, hoping that the use of the vernacular tongue would help to rally the sinking spirits of the people and to strengthen their feeling of national unity. Other less important writers followed his example, and the Sultan welcomed the innovation, though it was not until the Karamanoglu had installed themselves in Konya in 1327 that Turkish was used in the chanceleries and government departments. This change aroused the fierce opposition of the scribes, some of whom had to be put to death before the order could be enforced. The choice of Turkish as the official language also affected the school teachers, who were thereafter obliged to teach a rather different script to their pupils, but the Karamanoglu were so determined to see the reform enforced that they instructed the Turcoman poet, the Hoça Dahhani, a native of Horasan who spoke the same form of Turkish as had the Seljuks, to translate the *Shahnamah* into Turkish. The version he produced is so accomplished that there is reason to think that in his childhood the poet must have been nurtured on epics of the early Ghuzz, which are now lost to us. Thus the stand which the Mevlevi of Konya had taken against the Mongols preserved for future generations of Turks something of the spirit and outlook that had characterized the Seljuks.

THE TUGRA The superb beauty of Seljukid calligraphy may also have helped to keep the literary tradition alive during the days of the Mongol occupation and of the Beylıks which followed it. It also transmitted to future generations the fascinating design which, originating as a nomadic brand mark, became the emblem of the Ghuzz and eventually developed into the cipher or calligraphic device of the sultans of Ottoman Turkey. It retained to the last its original name of *tugra*. Malık Shah of Persia was probably the first to use it as his crest, having had it designed for him by the poet and calligrapher Mul'aiyid al Din Fakhr al Kuttab who succeeded the Nizam al Mulk as Vizir. The badge was so beautiful that the idea of using it as a crest caught on among the Islamic sovereigns, and the Mamluks of Egypt were the first to follow the example set by the Seljuks. In Asia Minor a special post was created at court, that of *Tugra Çekmet* or Maker of the Tugra, with which went the duty of preparing the rectangular pieces of paper on the space purˌposely left blank at the top of every state document; on these scribes later delineated the tugra, the design of which varied with each sultan. Soon no state document was valid unless it bore this emblem at its head.

The tugra always preserved its basic outline, and this shape is so curious that some people see in it the silhouette of a galloping horse, while others liken it to a bird. Linguists favour the second interpretation because they associate the word 'tugra' with the name of the fabulous bird whose picture appeared on the standards of the early Turkish Khakans. This theory is to some extent supported by a passage in the *Shah-namah* which says that 'the Khakan made a present of the bird to Bahram Gur', which experts in oriental heraldry are inclined to regard as a reference to a crest. Whether or not this was so, the tugra remains one of the finest calligraphic devices ever to have been evolved, and it is sad that no example dating back to Seljukid times has come down to us.

CHAPTER V

The Arts of Everyday

To gladden the heart of the weary, to remove the suffering
of the afflicted has its own reward.

A saying of Muhammad

To ASSESS CORRECTLY the significance of the Seljuks
it is essential to consider the quality and character of their
artistic achievement, for this represents their most enduring
legacy to posterity. Among the minor arts their ceramics and
calligraphy are of an unusually high order, but most important
is their architecture, and the sculptured and carved decorations
which are a part of it.

The imposing, rectilinear Seljukid buildings are almost classical in their uncompromising directness. Their calm assurance
is all the more astonishing when it is remembered that many
of them were built during the very years when the Seljuks were
fighting to retain their empire, while others were constructed
when the Mongols were in control of the sultanate and the
dynasty's life was running out. Even then, their passion for
building remained so strong that, in the year 1271, we see the
Seljukid Vizir Fakhreddin Husein Sahip Ata founding the
Gök Medrese at Sivas, while the Grand Vizir of the Mongol
Ilkhan of Persia was similarly occupied in founding the Çifte
Medrese in the same city.

Fig. 12

The majority of the buildings which survive in Asia Minor
fall into two groups. The larger of the two is made up of the
mosques, educational and charitable institutions and numerous
caravanserais with which the Seljuks endowed their empire;
the second comprise the mausolea which they set up to serve
both as mortuary chapels and as memorials to their dead. They
also constructed fortifications and palaces, as well as a great

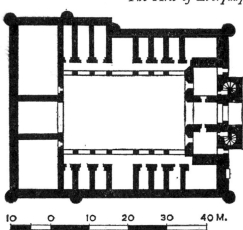

Fig. 12. Plan of the Gök Medrese, Sivas, 1271.

many public baths and fountains, and some magnificent
bridges, quite a number of which are still used regularly today.

The outlines of the buildings comprising the first group are
all surprisingly similar, for the majority are rectilinear, with
their outer walls faced with large blocks of dressed stone laid
with great accuracy, and all have their windows set high above
ground level; but whereas the windows of the mosques are not
unduly small, those of the caravanserais are little better than
slits.

These severe edifices are most remarkable for the attention
which their designers lavished on the main, often the only
entrance. They framed these doorways in several bands of varying widths of extremely ornate and intricate stone carving, disposed in such a manner as to transform the gateways into
monumental portals. Sometimes this decoration spills out on
either side of the entrance to adorn the greater part of the main
façade; but it is only rarely, as at Divriği or in the case of the
Gök Medrese at Sivas, that it is also to be found, if on a more
restrained scale, on the side walls and round the windows.
Even then, most of the decoration is concentrated round the

Plate 23

Fig. 13

Plate 12

131

Plate 11

main portal and on the minarets which complete the design of their ornate entrance gates, as for example on the Çifte Medrese at Erzurum and that of the same name at Sivas. In such cases the minarets are ornamented with bricks laid to form geometric patterns as well as with glazed tile and brick panels.

Fig. 13. Sculptured motif from the portal of Ak Han, Aksaray; 1250 to 1260.

THE
MOSQUE
AND THE
IVAN-
SHAPED
HALL

The Seljuks derived the basic features of their architecture from the Sasanians, who had in their turn inherited them from earlier civilizations. These elements comprise a square or rectilinear plan, a flat roof and a hall with a great horseshoe-shaped arch at one end of it, similar to that first used in the 8th century B.C. for Nebuchadnezzar's palace at Babylon, and known as the ivan hall. In Persian architecture this hall was flanked by smaller chambers, often disposed on two floors, four such wings being used to form a square or rectangle with a central courtyard. In pre-Islamic times the ivan hall was to be found in many parts of north-eastern Persia and even in Transoxiana, and it is there that the Seljuks may first have encountered it.

When the Seljuks acquired their faith from the Arabs they also took over from them the fundamental elements of mosque architecture. These did not conflict with the principles of the ivan-hall type of building to which they had become accus-tomed, for in Mesopotamia the Muslims had made the simple, rectangular, flat-roofed and many-columned hall of the Achae-menid audience chamber serve as the basis for the mosque. They did not elaborate the form till the construction of the Great Mosque of Damascus (706–715),[66] when certain features culled from Christian prototypes, such as the three-axial en-trance, the three-aisled sanctuary incorporating a wider central aisle, the use of transepts and columns, as well as the depen-dence on an open courtyard, became essential elements of mosque architecture.

Within another century and a half Ahmet ibn Tulun pro-vided a variant of this pillared kind of building in the form of the many-tiered, multi-arcaded type of mosque which is called after him and which still constitutes one of Cairo's greatest glories. In Asia Minor the Seljuks retained the ivan-shaped hall with which they had become familiar in Horasan, combining it with the rectilinear plan of the ancient and the Islamic worlds. They incorporated into it ibn Tulun's version of the many-piered type of interior, setting their numerous arches as hap-pily on columns, which are often of ancient date, as on oblong, square or rounded piers or imposts, deriving particular satisfac-tion from a complicated arrangement of intersecting arches. They were never hampered in this by any scarcity of good build-ing material, for northern Anatolia provided them, as still today, with unlimited supplies of excellent wood; western Anatolia also possessed rich marble deposits, and the flat

EVOLUTION OF ARCHI-TECTURAL STYLES

central plain furnished excellent limestone, as well as clay that was admirably suitable for the making of tiles and bricks.

The Seljuks were so pleased with the style they had evolved that they retained it practically unchanged to the end, merely concentrating upon refining its details. Because of this conservatism it is extremely difficult to assign a building to a particular year on stylistic grounds alone. The major differences that appear do so in the building's decorations, but often enough these are due to geographical factors or to the individual idiosyncrasies of their founders rather than to any difference in date. Time has always tended to slip by unnoticeably in the Orient, and this phenomenon in conjunction with the shortness of the Seljukid period could hardly be expected to produce any marked evolution of style. The absence of any such development should not be ascribed to ineptitude or indolence; it was the result of choice and not of incapacity.

The earliest surviving examples of Seljukid architecture, and these are among the finest and most original, are to be found on Persian soil, within the territory of the Great Seljuks, and thus do not concern us here. The style which the Seljuks produced in Rum differs in many respects from that which grew up in Persia. The buildings which survive in Asia Minor belong for the most part to the 13th century; a number date from the 12th and only a very few from the 11th century. Nor are all the 11th- and 12-century buildings strictly speaking Seljukid works, since certain of them were constructed by princes and notables who, although of Turkish origin and often even kinsmen or collateral relations of the Seljuks, were nevertheless their rivals. Such, for example, were the two Ortokid houses whose representatives ruled respectively in and around Harput and Malatya; the Saltukids, who were in control in Erzurum; the Menguçeks, whose monuments survive in and around Divriği, and the Danışmend, much of whose best work is to be seen at Kayseri. Yet the buildings erected by the

Fig. 14

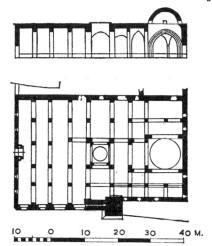

Fig. 14. Elevation and plan of the Ulu Cami, Kayseri, begun in 1135, completed in 1205.

10   0   10   20   30   40 M.

minor dynasties show only slight variations, primarily in the use and type of decoration, from the main development and, broadly speaking, all follow the same lines, for each was an offshoot of the style created by the Great Seljuks of Persia.

In Asia Minor it is possible by means of a careful study of the sculptured decorations, and sometimes too of the method of construction, to distinguish in Seljukid architecture a short opening period, lasting until 1210 or 1215 or so, which is seen for example in the Şifaiya or Giyasiye Medrese at Kayseri, generally known as the Çifte Medrese, founded in 1205 by Keyhüsrev I in honour of his sister Seljuka or Gevher Nesibi Hatun. This phase gave way to the fully-developed style which may be defined as the classical; this lasted till about 1250, and it includes such notable buildings as the Daruşşifa Hospital containing the mausoleum of Keykâvus I at Sivas (1217); the two Sultan Hans, dating respectively from 1229 and from 1230/31; the Huand Hatun foundation at Kayseri comprising a mosque containing her mausoleum, a medrese and a bath,

Plate 15

Figs. 8, 15

Fig. 10

135

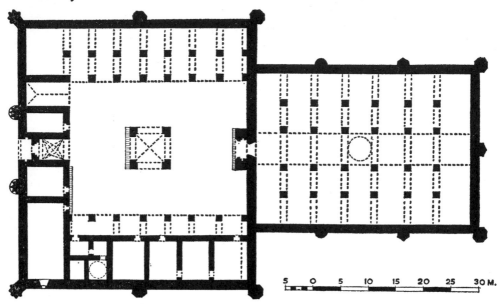

Fig. 15. Plan of the Sultan Han on the Kayseri–Sivas Road, 1230/31.

dating from 1237/38; and scores of others. Finally, there is the closing baroque phase, which is expressed in such buildings as the Ince Minareli Medrese at Konya, founded in 1258 by the Vizir Sahip Ata and built by Abdulla b Kelük, or the Gök Medrese of Sivas, founded by the same benefactor in 1271. This baroque style should not, however, be confused with that of the remarkable dual foundation of the cathedral mosque and mental hospital at Divriği. The latter was commissioned jointly in 1228 by Fatima Turan Melik, the daughter of Fahreddin Bahram Shah, and her husband Ahmet Shah, the Menguçek ruler of Divriği. It was built for them by Kuramshah of Gelat (Ahlat) and Ahmet ibn Ibrahim of Tiflis. It is so individualistic that it stands alone, and is better described as a flamboyant rather than a baroque work.

Plate 7

Plate 12, *Fig. 12*

Plate 39, *Fig. 16*

Fig. 6

136

In Asia Minor the Seljuks began, on capturing a town, by constructing an *Ulu Cami* or cathedral mosque. They seldom converted a Christian church for this use, as they were on the whole averse to interfering with the religious observances of the local population, but they made use of the largest church in the town while the Ulu Cami was being built, and retained the church thereafter to serve as an additional mosque. The position chosen for the Ulu Cami was always the most prominent, and this generally meant that an existing church had to be destroyed to make way for it.

The harsh climate of Asia Minor quickly convinced the Seljuks of the need to abandon the open courtyard type of mosque for an enclosed one, but they retained the square or rectangular plan of the earlier versions and, at first—as in the Ulu Cami of Kayseri, built by the Danışmend in 1135 but *Fig. 14* altered by the Seljuks somewhat later, or in the Saltukid

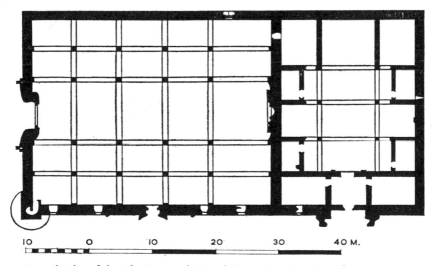

Fig. 16. Plan of the Ulu Cami and Mental Hospital at Divriği, 1228.

Ulu Cami at Erzurum built in 1179—they left an unroofed space in the centre of the mosque to recall the vanished court, yard. Rather later, although very rarely, an ablution fountain was placed inside a mosque beneath the central dome to represent the one which had originally occupied the centre of the courtyard. Gabriel[67] considers that the second, central dome of Kayseri's Ulu Cami, which is in line with the earlier dome raised before the *mihrab* or altar to indicate its axis, is a later addition, introduced to cover what was originally a central open, ing; he goes on to suggest that the same occurred in the cases of the Alaeddin Mosque at Nigde (1223), of the Huand Hatun

Plate 27   Mosque at Kayseri, and even of the Eşrefoglu Mosque at Beyşehir built as late as 1296–98, as well as in certain other instances.

TURKISH   The earlier mosques had flat roofs made of an earth filling
TRIANGLES   beaten into a foundation of rafters, with channels cut in it for
Plate 5   the rain and snow to run off. However, a flat dome was already in use in 1219, when the Ferguniye Cami at Konya was pro, vided with one. During the experimental stage the dome was generally built of bricks and covered on the outside either with lead or glazed tiles. Inside it was supported by squinches or pendentives of a peculiar triangular shape. These were first seen in the Chidsha Rabi near Meshed, built in 1026, but are now so firmly associated with Asia Minor that they are gener, ally known as Turkish triangles. The inside of the dome was decorated with tiles or glazed bricks, and the Turkish triangles on which it rested were often cut by a series of triangular

Plate 38   incisions producing a stalactite or honeycomb effect. This form of decoration was inspired by Persian plaster, work of the 11th century; by means of it the Seljuks succeeded in entirely altering the appearance not only of their squinches but also of their niches and alcoves. The form appears on Muslim buildings in Azerbaidzhan at an earlier date than in Asia Minor, as, for example, on the minaret of Sınık Kale at Batum, dated to 1079, but it is nevertheless one which, when rendered in stone, is to be primarily associated with the architecture of the Seljuks of Rum.

At first the building technique in Rum resembled that in Persia. Even in the 12th century, as in the mosque at Dunyaşir and in the Daruşşifa Hospital at Sivas, where the walls are faced on the outside with dressed stone, the inside reveals that they are made of brick, while the sultan's mausoleum, though tiled in the characteristic Anatolian manner, has arches that are Persian in shape; nor is this surprising when we find that at any rate one of the architects responsible for the work, Ahmet b Bizl, came from Maranda in Persia. More often, however, the walls of stone buildings were made of rubble or rough stone and then faced with large blocks of beautifully dressed and laid stones. In such Saltukid buildings as the Uli Cami of Erzurum and the great han at Tercan the lack of decoration allows the beauty of the masonry to be seen in its true splendour; the severity enhances the grandeur of the forms, and within, it produces an atmosphere of awe; this is achieved largely by the means of the veritable forest of piers and columns brought in to support the vaulted stone ceiling. In the earlier mosques the number of columns is relatively small, but forty-two of antique origin were re-used in the Alaeddin Mosque at Konya and ninety were employed in Sivas's Ulu Cami; the number decreased with Divriği's Ulu Cami, but even so, it is the multiplicity of columns and arcades which helps to the last to distinguish the Seljukid style from the Ottoman.

MASONRY
Plate 38

Plate 20

Today the minaret is regarded as an essential feature of Islamic architecture, yet the earliest Anatolian mosques were probably not equipped with them, the call to prayer being made, as originally in Arabia, from the highest roof in the neighbourhood. However the Iplıkçi Mosque at Konya,[68] though built

MINARETS
Plates 1, 7, 11

between 1162 and 1182, may well already have possessed a minaret, for the brick base of one was discovered during a recent restoration. It is probable that by the beginning of the 13th century all mosques of importance were supplied with this slender, Islamic form of tower which, together with the coni-cally-shaped roofs of the Seljukid mausolea, did more to trans-form the landscape of Byzantium than did any other feature of Muslim architecture. Immense trouble was taken to make the minaret as elegant, tall and decorative as possible. Unglazed bricks were laid up its shaft to form geometric patterns in order to stress its height, and its salient points were decorated and at the same time preserved from corrosion by a facing of glazed tiles or bricks.

MAUSOLEA
Plates 24–27,
31–36

The Seljukid *türbes* or *kümbets* as the mausolea are called have survived in considerable numbers; they are the most poetic of the Seljukid buildings and epitomize Seljukid virtuosity. In conception they are tribal and Central Asian rather than Is-lamic. They are of two types: the one type has a cylindrical tower which is shorter and broader than the pencil-pointed mortuary towers of northern Persia—though it is obviously an offshoot of these—and is roofed with a low flat dome, which, as in the Sırçalı Kümbet at Kayseri (1247/48), was sometimes covered on the outside with turquoise-coloured tiles; the other type is made up of a circular, polygonal or octagonal body fitted on to a square base by means of Turkish triangles, and roofed with a conically-shaped turret. Often these buildings carry an inscription, the flowing letters of which are carved with supreme skill; occasionally they are adorned with sculptures, but gener-ally they are left plain, in which case their beauty depends upon the quality of their masonry and proportions.

Both the türbes and the kümbets are generally two-storeyed structures. The lower floor served as a mortuary chapel; it con-tained the body lying in a stone coffin which was often inscribed and sometimes embellished with glazed tiles. A flight of external steps led to the upper chamber. This was fitted as a chapel and contained a *mihrab*, or altar, and generally also a commemorative inscription; its ceiling often took the form of a flat dome. One of the earliest türbes, built by the Danişmend in 1146 for Halifet Gazi at Amasya, is among the most graceful; a türbe at Tokat and a group of them at Van are especially Plates 32, 35 picturesque; the more ornate examples include the one erected for Melik Gazi at Kirşehir (1250), the Döner Kümbet at Plate 34 Kayseri (1276), the Turumtay türbe at Amasya (1279) and Plate 46 the Hudavend Hatun türbe at Nigde (1312). The façades of Plate 36 these four are decorated with figural and geometric sculptures of real quality, much of the carving being in fairly high relief; they prove that the Seljukid architects were as skilful with work on a small scale as on a large, and that their touch could be as light as monumental.

The striking similarity between the conical roofs of the türbes and those of some early Armenian church steeples has led to much discussion. Strzygowski and his followers maintain that the form was invented in Armenia, for it first appeared there in the 8th century and may well have existed as early as the 6th. It is, however, tempting to associate their shape rather with that of the tents belonging to the Central Asian nomads and the Kurds. Gertrude Bell's account[69] of these tents, which she saw still in use in the vicinity of Erzurum, closely corresponds to that given by Friar Rubruquis and to the drawings Plate 33 he left of them.[70] He was particularly fascinated by the designs with which the Mongols adorned the felt panels covering their roofs. These are to some extent reflected in the blind arcading decorating the roofs of such Seljukid stone structures as the türbe of the Çifte Medrese at Erzurum or the Döner kümbet at Plates 25, 34 Kayseri. Tents of this type probably existed in quite early times for the clay ossuaries in the shape of dwellings which were in use in Samarkand from the 5th century A.D. include some which reproduce the round tents or pointed reed huts of the period; these closely resemble the later tents though their pointed roofs are surmounted by an effigy of a human head instead of terminating in a smoke-hole.[71]

Ossuaries of this type continued to be used in Samarkand till the Islamic invasion, and may well have inspired the shape not only of the early Christian church towers of Armenia, but also of the Seljukid türbes and the cylindrical, pencil-pointed turret tombs of Muslim Horasan. If so, then it was the Persian burials which remained closer to the original source of inspiration than did the two others, and the Seljuks of Rum must have used them as a point of departure for their own mortuary buildings, whereas the Armenians may have been influenced more directly from Central Asia. In the 13th century the links between Asia Minor and the Caucasian area were sufficiently close to enable the artists of each to affect the other; that the influence was a two-way one is evident even in the Crimea, at Cherson, where the Christian masons often faced the walls of their churches with dressed stone handled and cut in the manner which had become customary in Anatolia.

SCHOOLS
AND
CHARI-
TABLE
INSTITU-
TIONS

Figs. 12, 17

Plate 25

In Asia Minor the educational and charitable institutions built at the expense of royal or private founders all followed a similar architectural pattern. All were rectangular in plan and the majority used as their basic features the great ivan-shaped hall and the horseshoe-shaped archway. One of these arches framed the entrance whilst the three others opened into the ivan-shaped halls set in the centre of each of the inner walls. The space between them was filled in with smaller rooms which, in the case of a *medrese*, were often arranged as two storeys. Sometimes the ivans reached to the roof, sometimes smaller chambers were built above them. Both the Sırçalı Medrese at Konya (1242) and the Çifte Medrese at Erzurum (1253) were two-storeyed buildings. Climatic conditions generally made it necessary for

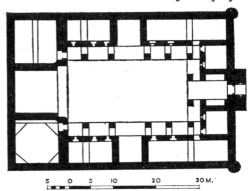

Fig. 17. Plan of the Sahibiye Medrese, Kayseri, 1267.

residential halls to be roofed over, but in the warmer regions a small area in the centre of the medrese was often left open and a fountain set in it which, with the help of the surrounding portico, gave the whole a cloister-like appearance. When the building was entirely roofed over the interior was lit by windows pierced in a central dome. The students' bedrooms were generally situated on the first floor; they were equipped with built-in fireplaces and cupboards. The ground floor housed the retiring rooms intended for the staff and the students' studies; the ivan-shaped halls were used for lectures. No kitchens were provided, and meals were sent in from outside.

This plan was used with only superficial modifications for the orphanages, poor house, *şifaiye* or hospitals and *bimarhaneler* or mental homes. Very occasionally, as in the case of Divriği, such institutions actually abutted on to the mosque forming part of the foundation. This somewhat unexpected combination may perhaps represent the final phase of a custom resulting from an order which had been given by the Caliph Umar after the theft of the public treasury from the governor's palace. In order to safeguard against future robberies, he suggested that the palace be rebuilt to adjoin the mosque, since 'the mosque has

Fig. 16

people in it day and night and they are the best safeguard of their treasure.'[72] In consequence throughout the next two cen~ turies it became customary in Iraq to build the governor's palace against the south side of a square mosque, and the practice may perhaps help to explain the construction at Divriği, after a lapse of several centuries, of a mosque and a hospital beneath one roof.

CARAVAN~
SERAIS
Plates 15, 20,
21

In Anatolia Seljukid architecture is to be seen at its most spectacular in the impressive ruins of the great caravanserais which still mark many of the old trade routes, once such busy thoroughfares. The majority of these establishments were built during the period of great expansion in commerce brought about by Keyhüsrev I, Keykâvus I and Keykûbad I, that is to say, between 1204 and 1246. They thus largely belong to the classical period. Some of the larger caravanserais were erected at the order of the sultans and these represent the imperial and metropolitan style.

Access to the caravanserais was gained in all cases by means of a single gate; it has been suggested that this peculiarity reproduces the single entrance of a nomad's tent, but it is far more likely that it was decided upon as a defence measure against raiders. The buildings were also safeguarded against attack by their extremely massive outer walls, which were further strengthened by towers at their corners, often along the main façades, and sometimes at regular intervals along all four walls as well. These walls were often built of uncut stone and then faced with large slabs of dressed stone, but sometimes they were entirely made of dressed stone. Occasionally stones from other buildings were re~used; more often they were newly quarried. The towers varied in shape; generally they were either square or rectangular, sometimes round or octagonal. The slit windows were set high in the walls, probably as an additional precaution against thieves.

The entrance gate or portal was lavishly adorned with bands Plate 15
of magnificently designed and carved stonework, its elegance
and sophistication heralding the urbane comforts awaiting the
weary traveller within. On crossing the threshold of such royal
foundations as the Sultan Hans (1229 and 1230), the traveller
would see first the tiny mosque occupying the centre of the Plate 16
square or rectangular courtyard, where it rose from a base Figs. 8, 15
formed by four high, horseshoe-shaped arches; thus poised, it
seems to float on air, so lightly was it held to earth on one side
only by an elegant external double staircase, framing the arch
fronting the gateway. With its delicate stone tracery the mosque
acquired the quality of a cabochon jewel of great price. In the
less sophisticated though equally well-built hans the mosque
was often placed either to the right of the porch or else immedi- Fig. 18
ately above it, when it was reached by an internal staircase.

The vaulted porch from which the traveller gazed upon the
courtyard was often flanked by the rooms provided for the

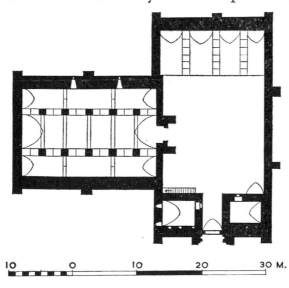

Fig. 18. Plan of Kesik Köprü Han near Kirşehir, 1268.

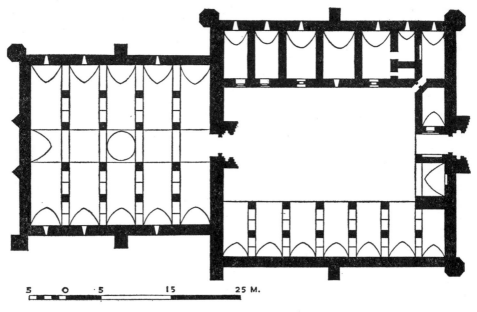

Fig. 19. Plan of Sarı Han on the Urgüp–Avanosa Road, 1238.

Plates 21, 22

han's porter and its staff; beyond these stretched the cloister‑like covered porticoes or open corridors leading on one side to the private bedrooms and dormitories, on the other to the baths, coffee‑room, kitchens, workshops and store‑rooms. The bedrooms were generally equipped with built‑in fireplaces, cup‑boards and couches, and were either on two floors or on the upper one only, when the lower one would provide additional storage space or stabling. Usually at the far end of the courtyard,

Figs. 8, 15, 19
Fig. 18

set opposite the entrance gate but sometimes situated instead at right angles to it, a second portal opened into a magnificent hall, with columns and piers arranged in rows to support transversal aisles with barrel‑vaulted ceilings. Of these the

Plate 19

central aisle was always the most impressive, for it generally contained a central dome, either round or conical in shape, pierced with windows. The body of the hall was poorly lit by tiny windows set at a great height. It was in these dim and splendid interiors that the animals were stabled beside built-in stone troughs, but it is tempting to think of them also being used in the cold winter months by the muleteers, for in magnificence they will stand comparison with any Oxford or Cambridge college dining-hall. The han at Tercan was provided with a kitchen as impressive as any produced at the same time in the West; its hearth is just as large as those in the kitchens at Fontevrault and at Glastonbury. Another of Tercan's refinements was the special stabling for camels; the horseshoe-shaped arch leading to their exceptionally high, vaulted quarters was infinitely loftier than those opening into the smaller stables provided for the horses and mules.

Fig. 7

The majority of the Anatolian towns which fell into Seljukid hands already possessed substantial fortifications, so that in most cases there was little need for the conquerors to do more than repair or strengthen them. Occasionally they added a buttress or tower to consolidate a weak spot, but careful study is necessary in order to distinguish these Seljukid additions from the earlier work, especially as the Seljukid sections were often built by the same local, probably Christian, workmen as had been employed by the Byzantines on the construction of the earlier defences. However, the Islamic inscriptions which the Seljuks set up and the monumental entrances which they added to many of the existing citadels must surely have been executed by Muslim rather than Greek hands. The town walls of Konya and Sivas were exceptional in that they were entirely built or wholly rebuilt at the order of Keykûbad I; however, all trace of them has now disappeared, and our knowledge of Seljukid fortifications is as a result largely dependent on what survives of the naval arsenal and land defences at Alaiye, and to a lesser extent, on the little that remains of the sea walls at

FORTIFICA-
TIONS

Plates 9, 28

Plate 10

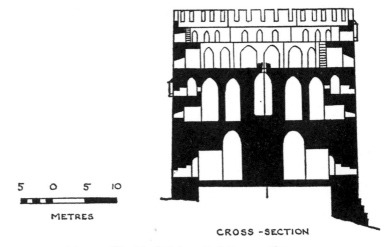

CROSS - SECTION

METRES

Fig. 20a. The Kızıl Kule or Red Tower, Alaiye, 1224.

Sinop. In their numerous wars the Seljuks had had ample opportunity to appreciate the strength of Syria's fortresses, and it may have been for this reason that Keykûbad I put a Syrian architect in charge of the work at Alaiye and at Sinop. At Alaiye the new defences required the extension of the existing fortifications and the redevelopment of the port. The new sys-
tem was made to hinge on a massive bastion, the Kızıl Kule or Red Tower, which was designed both to protect the large dockyard and to serve as a pivot for the new walls running up the western side of the hill, linking at the summit with the existing citadel and then swinging down to the sea. This mag-nificent octagonal tower was built round a central pier, the upper sections of which served as a water cistern. The tower contained five storeys: a ground floor, a first floor, a mezzanine floor, a top storey enclosed by battlements and a roof terrace, admirably conceived, each different in lay out. The space enclosed within the new walls was divided into six sectors. The most important and, indeed, unique feature of the scheme

Plate 29
Figs. 20a, 20b
Plate 30

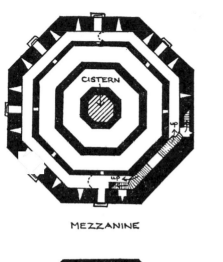

MEZZANINE

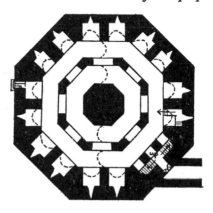

FIRST FLOOR

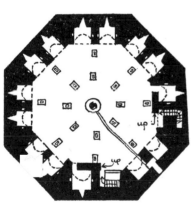

ROOF PLAN

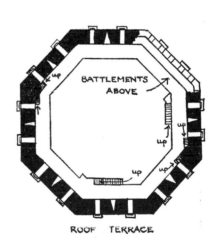

ROOF TERRACE

Fig. 20b. Floor and roof plans of the Kızıl Kule, Alaiye.

was the naval dockyard or *tersane* which was established on the southern side of the existing harbour. It was tunnelled into the cliff to a depth of 262 feet and contained within its 318-foot width five vaulted galleries. The side arches forming these galleries are of the characteristic horseshoe shape; their vaulted

Plate 30

Fig. 9

ceilings are of brick with special rounded spaces at their centre to enable quite large ships to lie concealed or even to be built in secret within their shelter. The façade is constructed of great blocks of ashlar carefully dressed and laid, and the work of the whole was so well carried out that the galleries are still used by the fishermen of Alaiye today.[73]

TOWN
LAYOUT

Fig. 21

The suburbs which sprang up round the remodelled port, like the new city of Konya and the towns which Keykûbad I established at Kubadabad, on the shore of the lake of Beyşehir, and at Kubadiye, near Kayseri, appear to have been more like the cities of Central Asia than those of Asia Minor. They covered a considerable area; houses alternated with markets and flower gardens, the streets contained conduits of running water, fountains and pools. Many of the fountains were built into the outer walls of the more important public buildings, when their shape recalled that of the typical Seljukid doorway. Public baths were regarded as essential and all towns were well provided with them; the majority were twin establishments, with one section for men and the other for women. Unlike the Roman bath, the Turkish bath of the Seljukid period was not equipped

Fig. 21. Fountain on the outer wall of
the Sahibiye Medrese, Kayseri, 1267.

with an immersion pool; instead the water flowed continuously from a tap or spout which was often inserted into a fountain, spilling into a basin.

In the smaller towns, at any rate at first, the market appears to have been held in the largest han. It may well be that the *bedestan,* or central pillared and vaulted portion, of the great covered bazaars of a later date—the section in which the jewellers' shops are now generally concentrated—developed as the result of this practice, and represents what survived of the original han when the market became so large that it engulfed the institution which had first given it hospitality.

A Seljukid manor house still survives on the outskirts of Kayseri, the only one of its kind to have done so. Built in 1251, it is known as Haidar Bey's Kiosk. The idea for a residence of this sort may just as well have reached the Seljuks from Central Asia as from Mesopotamia, for the Soghdian princes had possessed country castles from the 8th century onwards, while the Ummayads of Arabia had had them from an even earlier date. Central Asian castles such as that at Mug on the Upper Zaravsh[74] had the lower sections of their walls built of ashlar

HAIDAR
BEY'S
KIOSK
Figs. 5, 22

Fig. 22. The Haidar Bey Kiosk, Kayseri, 1251.

blocks, and the rooms within were given barrel-vaulted ceilings but mere slits of windows. The Haidar Bey Kiosk is built entirely of dressed stone. Basically a rectangular building, it abuts on to a defence tower which contains the entrance hall and an elegant stone staircase leading to the look-out tower. The rest of the building is single-storeyed, with the rooms ranged round a central court. Their ceilings are barrel-vaulted, and their windows are little more than slits, which leave the interior cool but far too dark. The lintels set above the doorways into the courtyard, together with the underside of the staircase, provided the only touch of decoration found in the Haidar Bey Kiosk.

Fig. 22

Fig. 23

Fig. 24

PALACES   With the exception of the Haidar Bey Kiosk no house of Seljukid date survives to throw light on the way in which these

Fig. 23. Fluting on the underside of the stone staircase in the Haidar Bey Kiosk.

Fig. 24. Lintel above a door leading to a room in the Haidar Bey Kiosk.

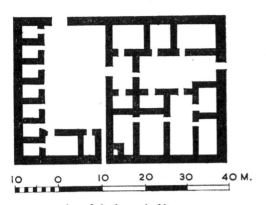

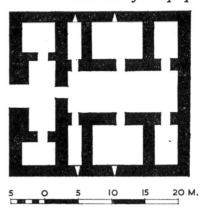

Fig. 25. Plan of the larger building at Kubadabad, 1235.

Fig. 26. Plan of the smaller building at Kubadabad, 1235.

early Turks adapted themselves to urban life. It was not until the 13th century that the sultans began to build palaces. Some of these were situated far from the capital, in settings chosen for reasons of climate, since some were intended as winter and others as summer residences. Certain scholars see in this a reflection of the Turks' ingrained desire for seasonal migration, but, when all is said and done, this practice is not peculiar to the Turks. Some of these palaces, like that of Sivas, are known only by name; the sites of others, like those of Alaiye and Antalya, have been identified; and the palaces which Keykû-bad I built and called after himself at Kubadabad and Kuba-diye between the years 1220 and 1235 have recently been excavated. Though the detailed result of the work still awaits publication, the plans of both the larger and the smaller resi-dences at Kubadabad show that they were rectilinear in shape and contained rooms opening on to courtyards.

Figs. 25, 26

Konya, as the capital, undoubtedly contained what was best and most characteristic of the period, and it is sad that so much

KONYA'S
CITADEL

153

Plate 10

Plate 4

Plate 3

has perished there in modern times. When Laborde visited the town in the 1830's he was able to make detailed drawings of the citadel.[75] Thirty years later both the citadel and the outer walls were still there for Texier to study;[76] he found that the town was in the shape of a rectangle with its corners rounded off; a hundred and eight great stone towers set some 46 feet apart along its walls were still standing; each measured some 32 feet wide by 26 feet deep. The citadel was situated in the centre of the town, enclosing the hillock on which the Alaed-din Mosque stands and the palace had become established. Examining the citadel at the end of the last century Huart[77] found that it was in the shape of a pentagon and that one of its inscriptions bore the date 1214. The first mosque had been begun by Sultan Mesud (1116–56) and completed under Kılıçarslan II, whose türbe—the work of Yusuf b Abdulgaffar of Hoçan—dates from 1188. In 1219 Keykâvus I entrusted the rebuilding of this mosque to the Syrian architect, Muhammad ibn Kaulan of Damascus, who employed as his foreman Ayaz Atabeki; and it was to the mausoleum which now contains the coffins of eight Seljukid sultans that Keykâvus had brought his father's body for reburial after Theodore Lascaris had paid tribute to his fallen foe. However, it fell to Keykâvus's brother, Keykûbad I, to complete in 1220 the mosque which now bears his name. Its final plan closely resembles that of such notable edifices as the Great Mosque of Damascus, the ibn Tulun Mosque at Cairo and that of Cordova, retaining the flat roof characteristic of these earlier works.

The two impressive towers which contained the two main entrances to Konya's citadel were erected at the expense of Keykûbad I in 1221; his munificence was recorded in letters of gold emblazoned upon these gates. He encouraged the local notables to make themselves similarly responsible for some of the other towers, arranging for the names of those who did so to be recorded upon the sections of the walls which had been built at their cost. On his own sections he expressed his delight in the *Shahnamah* as well as in figural sculpture by having quotations from the former inscribed where all could read them, and having sculptured stones of various sorts set into both his gateways. Some of the sculptures were of Hellenistic, others of Byzantine workmanship. They included the sarcophagus decorated with scenes showing Alexander in Skiros which is now preserved in the Museum of Sculpture at Konya, as well as over twenty figures of lions and several of eagles, many of which were actually Seljukid works. Most interesting among these were two pairs of winged genii or angels set in pairs very prominently above each entrance. Though some of these sculptures have been preserved, nothing now remains of the walls or gateways, and only a few stones survive of the palace buildings which stretched from the main gate almost to the wall of the Alaeddin Mosque.

Plate 10

Plates 50, 54, 62

Yet in Texier's day one pavilion, known as the Kiosk, still remained. Then in 1906 an earthquake destroyed the greater part of it. Nevertheless, when Sarre visited Konya shortly afterwards[78] the walls of one end were still standing to a height of some 50 feet and a length of 32 feet or so. From Texier's and Sarre's records it is evident that the Kiosk was originally an important two-storeyed structure, built of the local brick which had an admixture of chalk, and set in a cement with a chalk basis. Its upper storey contained a large oblong hall with a balcony at one end and windows on either side; two of these survived the 1906 earthquake on each of the lateral walls; they were set in blind arcades of horseshoe shape, and a larger arch of the same shape, but with an inscription set above it, framed the doorway giving on to the balcony. Sarre associates the inscription with Kılıçarslan IV and therefore dates the Kiosk to between the years 1246 and 1264.

In Sarre's day the ceiling had fallen, but Texier had been able to gaze on it and delight in its elaborate painted decoration,

THE KIOSK

Plate 2

which appears to have resembled that adorning the Capella Palatina at Palermo. When Sarre examined the building its balcony had collapsed, but the supporting struts were still in place at a height of 29 feet from the ground; they were carved on the underside into stalactite-shaped incisions, giving a honeycomb effect, and traces of their painted decoration could still be distinguished. The inscription above the balcony door still retained some of the blue and white tiles from which it was made; fragments of plaster work of both a geometric and a figural character and some star-shaped glazed tiles remained in place on the upper sections of the walls; below, there were still portions of marble revetments, and a sculptured lion set in a niche continued to mount guard over the ruin. Some of these fragments are now in Konya's museums; gazing at them it is difficult to remember that this ornate and elegant pavilion was built during the very years when the Mongols were in control of Seljukid affairs and when each of the three brothers linked in the triumvirate which ostensibly ruled the country was scheming to become sole sovereign.

CHAPTER VI

The Minor Arts

These are our works; these works our souls display.
Behold our works when we have passed away.[79]

THE SELJUKS DELIGHTED in decoration. A wise instinct led them strictly to limit its use, but on the surfaces
which they reserved for it they produced a riot of pattern, and
their artists often tended to be more preoccupied with this
aspect of their work than they were concerned with matters
affecting form. This idiosyncrasy does not detract from the
quality of the finished product, but it does endow it with a
character entirely its own.

The style of Seljukid carving, regardless of whether it was
carried out in stone, stucco or wood, displays in its conception
close affinities with the plaster-work decorations produced at an
earlier date both in Persia and in Mesopotamia, but the actual
manner of its execution appears to suggest a closer familiarity
with the technique of wood-carving than with that of working
stucco or stone. The way in which it is applied seems to reflect
the Asiatic tribesman's immemorially-old appreciation of textiles as wall hangings;[80] it was this which made them concentrate their sculptures round the great portals of their buildings,
and later, under Persian and Byzantine influence, also around
the windows and along the tops of their walls, so that the
decorated stones showed up against the unadorned façades in
much the same way as a hanging or rug stands out when
placed against a bare wall. The contrast formed by the jux-
taposition of plain and ornate surfaces emerges with all the
sharpness which distinguishes light and shade in the brilliant
sunlight of the Orient, where natural conditions teach the eye
to delight in these differences; indeed, the Seljuks seem to have

taken particular pleasure in it, tending with the years to stress it by deepening the relief of their carving. In Konya under Keykûbad I, when Syrian influence was to the fore, this effect was often achieved by the use of two shades of stone or marble *Fig. 11* rather than by undercutting—the lintel above the doorway set into the wall of the Alaeddin Mosque at Konya and the portal of Zazadin Han (1234/35) are in this style. The style was never put into wide use, but it is to be found here and there throughout Rum, reappearing at Konya, in 1251, in the *Plate 6* entrance to the Büyük Karatay Medrese. Yet even when this Syrian characteristic breaks through, the predominating influence remained Persian rather than Syrian, Central Asian quite as much as Arabian. It is in the tomb of Ismail of Saman at Buhara (died 907) that decorative bandwork and medallions were perhaps first associated on the façade of a building.

FIRST
PERIOD
The extent to which decoration was used no less than its character helps to mark the three stages of evolution of the Seljukid style. In the first or opening phase, which includes such important buildings as the Alaeddin Mosque at Konya and the Altınapa and Onü hans, both built in 1201, the decorated areas are strictly limited and their style is sober and restrained. Persian influence is responsible for the stalactite type of decoration as well as for the shape of the niches set on either side of *Plates 17, 46* many a portal, and also for such motifs as the palmette and rosette. The Seljuks combined these Persian designs with others which, depending upon the geographical disposition of their own cities, they culled either from Central Asian or from Western sources; to the former belong many of the axe-head-

Fig. 27. Motif from the decorations on the mausoleum of the Vizir Sahip Ata, Konya, 1282.

like shapes, the triangular patterns or the angular or geometric trilobal borders or bands, as well as some of the basket plaits; to the latter, the pilasters and capitals which flank many a Seljukid doorway, and patterns such as the zigzag, Greek key or the dog tooth. In the earlier stage, designs of both types are

Fig. 13

Plate 44

Fig. 27

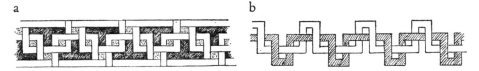

Fig. 28. Variants of the Greek Key motif: a. From Sırçal Medrese, Konya, 1242/43. b. From Büyük Karatay Medrese, Konya, 1251.

tentative and simple, and, except at Kayseri, they are in low relief. Some of the medallions contain single floral motifs which, though primarily Persian in character, may also well be of Chinese origin. The arabesque also makes its appearance; indeed this device, which was among those used by ibn Tulun, soon came to figure as prominently in Seljukid decoration as Persian motifs, its popularity being doubtless encouraged by its frequent use in the metalwork of the period. It was combined with a series of designs which stem from the Caucasian area[81] and, at Divriği, a Caucasian architect and designer was even employed.

Plate 17

The classical or second period in Seljukid art lasted for only some thirty-five years, but it comprises many of their greatest buildings. These include both Sultan Hans as well as Karatay Han (1240/41), in all of which the size of the decorated surfaces was increased till these areas became of supreme importance, the elaborate tracery of their sculpture producing a lace-like effect. Arabesques now vied with designs of Persian origin, but at the same time they themselves acquired a Persian veneer by means of the minute animal or floral motifs which occupied

SECOND
PERIOD
Plate 15

Plate 43

Plates 11-14

the tiny areas left bare by their convolutions. Naturally enough it was in Konya that the metropolitan style produced the most sophisticated results, while the best of the regional works were created at Sivas and Kayseri.

Plate 4

Plate 6

The transition from the opening phase, as represented in the Alaeddin Mosque at Konya, to the fully-developed classical style is perhaps to be seen at its clearest in the façade of the Büyük Karatay Medrese at Konya. Here the sobriety of the earlier phase is reflected in the tympanum, but the doorway has been recessed to allow for the insertion of pointed, honey-combed arches of typically Seljukid type, whilst lateral pilasters and capitals of classical inspiration appear for purely decorative reasons. Seljukid artists often disregarded the architectural functions of these features, using them as a means of carrying the eye upwards or of emphasizing the rectilinear character of their style.

In the portal of the Karatay Medrese the rhythm of the basic decoration is to some extent broken by the introduction of three deeply undercut medallions or bosses. These are characteristic of the style and often make a somewhat incongruous appearance on a monument. Some authorities trace their presence on Seljukid buildings to the influence of Byzantine metalwork, but others regard it as a variant of the Babylonian habit of decorating the façades of buildings with inset glazed plaques. The most likely explanation of the bosses would seem, however, to lie in Artin Pacha's observation[82] that the earliest crests in use in the Orient appeared on the round shields carried by the tribal chieftains and Islamic princes, and that when it eventually became customary to display these personal crests or cyphers on the holder's house or portable possessions, the device was shown on a roundel representing the shield on which it had first been emblazoned. If this is so,

Plate 39

a detailed study of the earliest bosses may well reveal debased renderings of heraldic devices.

The portal of the Sırçalı Medrese at Konya (1242) is of much the same date as the Karatay Medrese, but the eastern imprint is more in evidence. This is scarcely surprising, for one of its architects, who is known both as Muhammad and also as Osman ibn Mehmet, when inscribing his name on the building, proudly added that he came from Tus.

In the Sahip Ata or Larende Mosque portal at Konya (1258), the work of Abdulla b Kelük, and the Çifte Medrese at Sivas (1271), the stalactite-topped niches, the rather flat though still cabochon-shaped roundels, the glazed tile work and the extreme elaboration of the sculpture heralds the third and final stage in the art—the baroque phase. The decorative sculpture work on the Ulu Cami and mental hospital at Divriği, dating from 1228, is flamboyant, eclectic and somewhat barbaric in its primitive exuberance. The Asiatic element is particularly marked in the decoration of its capitals (a) though it is perhaps more easily appreciated by comparing the motif adorning one of the columns in the hospital (b) to a very similar design of the classical period from Sultan Han (c). At Divriği, the influence of the stucco work of Hamadan is combined with that of such buildings as the Rabat-i-Malık near Buhara (1050–80) or of the Gumbat-i-Surkh at Maragha (1147), but, in addition, the style also reflects Hindu taste in the decoration of its bosses, and touches of Indian jewellery in the half-moon motifs which play a recurrent role in its decoration.

In Amasya where much of the decoration is derived from Horasanian and Caucasian patterns there was a tendency to concentrate a single motif on a chosen spot, repeating it till it developed into a decorative panel reminiscent in its effect of that of glazed tiles; a good example of this style is to be seen on the Turumtay türbe. At Kayseri Caucasian patterns are to the fore, and also to some extent at Sivas. The artists of Kayseri were particularly fond of massive geometric compositions and

THIRD
PERIOD
Plate 11

Plates 39, 40, 41
Figs. 29a to e

Plates 39, 40, 41

Plate 46

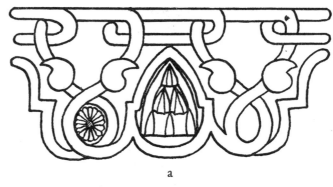

a

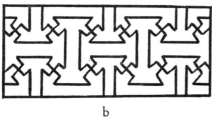

b

c

d

e

Fig. 29. Sculptured motifs from the Ulu Cami and Mental Hospital at Divriği, 1228/29. a. A capital. b. Decoration from a column. Next to it, for comparison, is shown c. a motif from the Konya-Aksaray Sultan Han, 1229; d. arabesque and crescent motif; e. geometric motif of floral inspiration.

of menanders, associating both with elaborate arabesques, using *Figs. 30a and b* these decorations both to stress certain structural features such as the bases of the minarets, windows and portals and also to form friezes. They likewise often combined them, as in the Döner kümbet, with animal and floral motifs. But although Plates 34, 36 many of the basket bands, plaits and frets probably reached both Kayseri and Divriği from the Caucasian area, they must *Fig. 31* in the first instance have been evolved in Horasan, for they reproduce in stone a form of decoration which essentially belongs to brickwork.

a

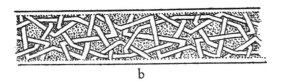

b

Fig. 30. a. 13th-century carved wooden door. Geometric patterns combined with arabesques, c. 1 m. 70 cm. by 90 cm.; b. Geometric pattern derived from Kufic script from the Büyük Karatay Medrese, Konya, 1251

In Sivas bandwork generally takes the form of parallel strips BANDWORK rather than of the broken or interlaced shapes of Caucasian Plate 14 character. However, the ribbon-like bands which adorn the Plate 8

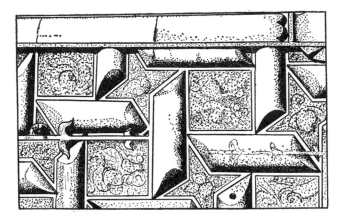

Fig. 31. Sculptured motif from the Ulu Cami, Divriği, 1228/29.

baroque portal of Ince Minareli Medrese at Konya (1258), another example of the work of Abdulla b Kelük, are altogether different from either of these types; they seem to be linked rather to some of the brickwork which appears on certain Abbasid buildings in Mesopotamia and on such Ummayad palaces as the Kherbet al Ma'fja, or again on such Coptic churches as that of Deir es-Suriani in Lower Egypt. The latter was founded by Bishop Moses of Nisibin in the 10th century and its decoration is in the same high relief as that of Ince Medrese; in addition it has so much in common both with the sculptures of the Ulu Cami at Divriği and of the Tower of Mahmud at Ghazna that it is scarcely possible to exclude the probability that Central Asian ideas penetrated as far as Egypt.

DECORA-
TIVE
MOTIFS
Fig. 32
Figs. 33a and b

Another motif, the vine scroll, may likewise have reached the Seljuks from the east rather than the west, since it appeared in Mazdean art from quite an early date, figuring in it as the symbol of the Hvarenah.[83] A more characteristic design is that of the tulip, though it may equally well be a variant of the lotus. Amidst all these constantly recurring shapes, some of

Fig. 32. Vine-leaf scroll from the Büyük Karatay Medrese, Konya, 1251.

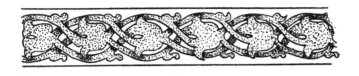

a

b

Fig. 33. Variants of the tulip or lotus motif; a. from a carved wooden door of the 13th century in the Çinli Kiosk, Istanbul; b. from the Konya-Aksaray Sultan Han, 1229.

Fig. 34. The two-lobed leaf motif.

them peculiar to the east, others to the west, and still others shared by the ancient civilizations of the Orient, one predominating motif can be considered essentially Seljukid. It appears to have been evolved by them and then used by their artists so frequently and so widely that it can be regarded as the hall-mark of their workmanship. This design consists of a flattened, more often than not two-lobed leaf. Sometimes a third lobe protrudes at its centre. In either case one of the side lobes is invariably extended to form an elongated point. The motif is

Fig. 34

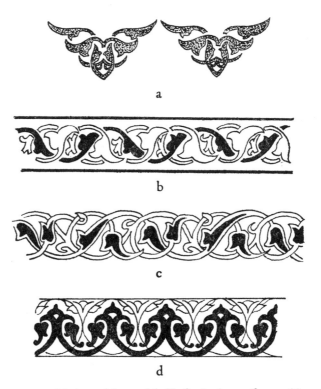

*Fig. 35. Variants of the two-lobed leaf and tulip motifs: a. and b.
from Sırçalı Medrese, Konya, 1242; c. and d. from the Alaeddin
Mosque, Konya, 1219/20.*

Figs. 35a, b, c, d
Figs. 36–38

Fig. 3
Fig. 39

used to produce scrolls or single devices, or to furnish the
elements for an elaborate design, or to form a terminal—it is
even employed to finish off the handles of the two swords in
the Koyunoglu collection. Like the Celtic and the Anglo-
Saxon decorative artists in Britain, the Seljuks could delineate
the most complicated designs freehand, weaving every element
in their repertory into intricate repeat patterns; they drew them
without the aid of mathematical instruments, often producing
asymmetrical designs.

Fig. 36. Glazed tile from the Sahip Ata Mausoleum, Konya, 1282, containing the two-lobed leaf motif, c. 18 cm. by 12 cm.

Fig. 37. Mosaic tile in two shades of blue from the Sırçalı Medrese, Konya, 1242. Width c. 10 cm.

Fig. 38. A tile showing the two-lobed leaf motif, c. 20 cm. by 30 cm.

Fig. 39. Glazed tile displaying characteristic motifs, c. 20 cm. by 20 cm.

SYMBOLIC
FORMS
Fig. 41

Figs. 40, 42

In the Seljukid age many ancient shapes continued to retain their symbolic significance largely because they still figured in astrology, and this probably helps to explain the frequency with which they occur in the art of the period. Stars with from five to twelve points constantly appear, figuring even on the

Fig. 40. Glazed tile showing a star set in an octagon intersected by interlaced bands, c. 72 cm. by 20 cm.

Fig. 41. Swastika- and diamond-shaped motif from the façade of Sırçalı Medrese, Konya, 1242.

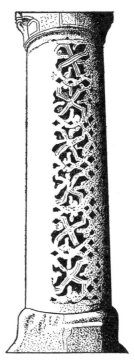

Fig. 42. Column from the Çifte Medrese, Erzurum, partially carved with a star design, 1253.

coins, where they may have represented Venus. In astrology Venus personified goodness and renewed life. When combined with a crescent they may have signified Venus' meeting with the moon. On the other hand, certain passages in the *Shahnamah* suggest that representations of the sun and moon had a political

Plates 79, 80

rather than a magical meaning, for Kay Khusraw, whose violet banner displayed both orbs, remarked that he had heard 'the Mobeds say that when the Moon of the Turans [the Turks] reaches its zenith it will be vanquished by the sun of Iran'; it may, therefore, not be due entirely to chance that sculptures of the sun and moon are generally set at the same height, as is the case, for example, in the Daruşşifa Hospital at Sivas, or at Ak Han.

Plate 45

ANIMAL FORMS IN DECORA-TION

Plates 42–44, 49–59

Fig. 43

The persistency with which animal forms recur in Seljukid decoration may well represent a last flicker of the animal art which had flourished from time immemorial in Central Asia and the ancient Orient. The stag is definitely to be associated with the art of the Scythian and Altaian nomads, especially when it is shown in the recumbent position, as on the plaque set above the doorway of the 13th-century Göregi Büyük Tekkesi at Niksar.[84] So, too, certain scrolls which at first glance

Fig. 43. Sculpture of a recumbent stag set above the door of Göregi Büyük Tekkesi, Niksar.

Figs. 44a and b

Plates 49, 50, 52

appear to be derived from floral compositions, may well in fact have been inspired by combat scenes from the animal art of the same regions.[85] On the other hand, eagles, lions and pos-sibly also falcons, though they can be paralleled in the art of these regions, are more likely to owe their presence in Seljukid decoration primarily to heraldic or symbolic considerations. The lion represented power, courage and noble lineage, and many a Seljuk incorporated the word for lion (*arslan*) into his

name in order to associate himself with these qualities. The lion was a frequently-used subject in Seljukid art. In sculptures it is to be found in a variety of styles: some works recall Hittite prototypes; others, such as the early statue from the citadel at Divriği, come closer to a Scythian source;[86] others again are essentially Hellenistic. But the Seljukid animals often retain the dot and comma or comma markings which characterize Altaian art.

Seljukid variants of these markings appear also on other animals, as on the caparisoned elephant which once adorned Konya's citadel. Occasionally zoomorphic junctures conforming to the Scythian tradition also appear; sometimes these begin with the contours of a leaf, then terminate in some animal attribute such as the tail of a fish, or else turn into the Seljukid two-lobed leaf motif, or into the head of another animal. These junctures occur most frequently on renderings of dragons.

Dragons such as that depicted on the Karatay Museum's sculptured stone slab are not uncommon in either Seljukid or Islamic art. Their popularity in Rum may have been partly due to the influence of Christian painting, but a more likely explanation is perhaps to be found in a passage in the *Shah-namah* in which Firdausi presents the beast as the symbol of

Plate 59
Fig. 45

Plate 57

Fig. 45. Stone sculpture of a griffin with its wings terminating in a fish's tail. Overall measurement, 1 m. by 80 cm.

the warring Turk by comparing the latter to 'a dangerous dragon whose breath is as fire and whose anger is like unto a tempest which rains down misfortunes'. It was in this spirit that, in 1227, the Caliph Nasir had himself depicted, in a sculpture set above the Talisman Gate at Baghdad, strangling two dragons, one of which represented the Mongols and the other the Shah of Kwarazm, both of whom were his enemies.

Plates 52, 53, 54, 55   Eagles are almost as common as lions in Seljukid art for they also served as symbols of royalty. They took the form of either single- or double-headed creatures with the faces either of eagles, lions or griffins. Some of the sculptured versions are strongly stylized and retain the dot and comma markings of an earlier age; others are more naturalistic; still others are close to Byzantine models.

FIGURAL SCULP- TURES   Many of the Seljukid carvings of animals are works of true artistry; the same is rarely true of their figural sculptures, though it does apply to their renderings of the human figure as it appears on the best of their pottery. The most remarkable of the figural sculptures are the larger pair of winged genii which were set above the main entrance to Konya's citadel. The idea for these could have come equally well from a Sasanian or a Roman source, but it is more likely that it emanated from the pair of winged victories which were set above the great Gate of the Kynigion at Constantinople, where they made an immediate impact on those arriving at the city, and must have impressed many visiting Seljuks. The genii are quite accomplished carvings, but most of the other figural works seem to have been produced by craftsmen rather than by artists. The majority are narrative, like a slab from the Museum of Turkish and Islamic Art at Istanbul showing two warriors wearing the type of chain mail and the pointed helms ascribed to the Seljuks by Firdausi.

A curious slab in the Ince Minare Museum at Konya is more intriguing; it shows a man seated on a folding stool, holding a hawk on one gloved hand and touching the cheek of a diminutive personage with the other; it probably represents a king speaking to a favourite retainer; the shape of the stone recalls that of a Roman stele. More Eastern in conception is a work showing a man seated cross-legged, holding a round object in one hand. The subject is not an uncommon one in Islamic art, stemming from a Sasanian source. Kühnel[87] has shown that the Caliph Muctadim (907–932) associated a figure of this type with one of a lute-player by using each to decorate a side of one of his coins; by Seljukid times both the origin of the figure and its Sasanian form, in which a seated figure is shown holding a cup in one hand, had been forgotten and the Sasanian cup had been replaced by a round object which some people identify as an apple. It is curious that neither the figure on this Anatolian stone nor any that appears in sculpture of this period is turbanned, even though special wool was imported at the time for the turbans worn by the sultan and his ministers of state. The costume reproduced by

Plate 62

Plate 61

Plate 58

Plate 60

Figs. 46, 47

Seljukid artists is closer to that worn by the 19th-century Kirghiz than that of the medieval Persians, and it may well be that in Asia Minor only the upper classes of the period dressed in the Persian style, while the average Seljuk retained the dress peculiar to the eastern Turks.

Fig. 46. Figure from a star-shaped tile from the site of the palace at Konya, showing the costume of the period, c. 7 cm. by 6 cm.

Fig. 47. Fragment of a glazed tile from the palace at Konya illustrating a robe of a different type from that shown in Fig. 46. Length c. 7 cm.

Plate 63

Recently the Islamic Department of the Berlin Museum acquired a Seljukid sculpture of a lute-player which is more accomplished than any other known figural work of the same origin. It is in marble and is reputed to have come from Anatolia, though the exact place of its origin has not been divulged. Kühnel has shown that lute-players were a popular subject in the Islamic world from Sasanian times onwards. In the Middle Ages they appeared in the Fatimid art of Egypt no less than in that of Turkestan, and they also formed a favourite motif of the so-called Mosul metal-workers and figured in the paintings of the Capella Palatina at Palermo. Figures of musicians are often found on the pottery of the Seljukid period in Persia and Anatolia. In sculpture, this Anatolian work is not only unique, but also remarkable for the sensitivity of its treatment and modelling.

Equally skilled renderings of people are often found on the fragments of stucco and pottery from Kubadabad and the site of Konya's palace; many of these are now exhibited in the Karatay Museum, Konya. More unusual is a spouted vessel from the Ethnographical Museum at Ankara which is adorned with roundels bearing figures which are in no way inferior to those found on Persian pots of the same date. Its paste distinguishes it from the Persian wares and the style of its figural decoration, for all its superficial resemblance to the Persian, is also sufficiently distinct to be recognizably Anatolian. Pottery intended for daily use was coarser in quality. A bowl in the museum at Kayseri shows that it had little affinity with anything that was being made at the time in Persia; the glazes, colouring and general technique are closer to the rougher types of wares which were then being produced in the Byzantine world to meet the need of the poorer people.

Plate 75

Figs. 51, 52

Fig. 48

Plate 74

Fig. 48. Pottery vessel with figures of men of Uygur appearance.

WOOD-
CARVING
AND
STUCCO
Fig. 49
Plates 66-68

Carved wood and decorative stucco were also important in interior decoration. The designs cut on the wooden shutters and doors are similar to those with which the stonemasons adorned their buildings. In the mosques the wooden *mimbers* or pulpits were also often worked with equally intricate patterns. The earliest and perhaps the finest of these is the ebony pulpit which Haci Menguberti carved in 1155 for Konya's first citadel mosque. Menguberti came from Ahlat and his style is not unlike that of the rather earlier carvings which survive in many parts of Georgia and Armenia; but this should not necessarily be taken to mean that the craft became established in the Caucasian area before it did so in Asia Minor. In both it probably stemmed from a common, possibly a Central Asian

Fig. 49. A motif from the carved mimber of the Ulu Cami, Divriği.

Fig. 50. A glazed tile with plaster insets from the mausoleum of Kılıçarslan II, Konya, c. 1192. Width c. 10 cm.

source, developing almost simultaneously in each area, but doing so on distinct though often parallel lines.

The mihrabs, also, provided artists with the opportunity to display their skill. The finest were made either of stucco or glazed tiles, or of the two combined, the stuccoed sections being carved and shaped to form stalactite-niches or delicate arabesque and geometric shapes reminiscent in style of Persian or Arabian work. Koranic inscriptions of great loveliness were incorporated in the decorations. The style of this type of stucco work is altogether different from that on the friezes and revetment plaques produced for Keykûbad's palaces. The latter were obviously for secular decoration, and animal and human forms were therefore allowed to predominate on them. Though many of these figures are small, all are monumental in character, recalling in their treatment the large stucco panel showing horsemen attacking each other and pursuing lions and dragons which was formerly on view in the Museum of Antiquities in Istanbul.[88]

Many of the tiled mihrabs are exceedingly beautiful. Among the finest is that which still stands in the Alaeddin Mosque in

Fig. 50
Plate 69

Konya; it is also the earliest of its kind. Its outer border is formed of tile mosaic work carried out in three shades of blue; its lovely *nakshi* inscription stands out clearly from a turquoise-blue ground, and its superb Kufic text from a dark blue one. The mihrab may well be the work of Kerimeddin Erdim Shah, who was also responsible for the mosque's dome and whose name figures in one of the mosque's inscriptions. The mihrab in Gülük Cami at Kayseri (1210) is of the same high quality, and even the later tile work in the Sahip Ata Mosque at Konya (1258/59) has lost none of its excellence with the passage of time.

Plate 69

GLAZED
TILES
Plate 5
Fig. 50

Figs. 46, 47, 51,
52

The Seljuks excelled at the difficult technique of producing glazed tiles and bricks, and used them with great skill to cover large areas on the insides and also on the outsides of their buildings. The tiles for their religious edifices were either plain turquoise blue or else carried star-shaped or floral motifs, but those intended for secular purposes often displayed human or animal figures. The Seljuks probably learnt to make tiles from

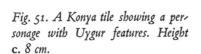

Fig. 51. A Konya tile showing a personage with Uygur features. Height c. 8 cm.

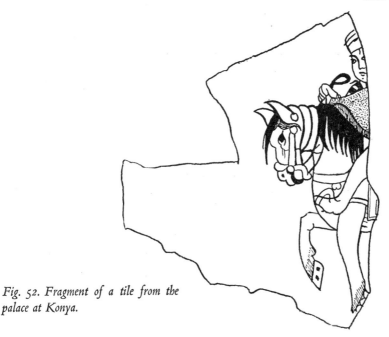

Fig. 52. Fragment of a tile from the palace at Konya.

the Persians, but in Asia Minor they worked independently, using a clay made up on a silicum basis. They limited their colours to three principal shades of blue, that is, to a very dark, almost black tone, to an indigo and to a turquoise, all three of which varied considerably in intensity. They also made use of much white, some dark brown, a little pink and an occasional yellow, which in the royal residences was often replaced by gold.

In the Middle Ages these colours served as political emblems throughout the Islamic world. According to the *Shahnamah* blues varying in shade from turquoise to lapiz were used as the national colour of Persia; black and a very dark shade of brown served as the emblem both of the Ghuzz and of the Abbasids, while white was associated with the Ummayads and the person of the Prophet,[89] for it was not till much

179

later that it was replaced by green, which then became the insignia of those who could trace their descent back to Muhammad or who had completed the pilgrimage to Mecca. Since it is unlikely that the small colour-range of the Seljukid potter's palette was due to any lack of technical skill it is tempting to ascribe it to the survival of this code of colour symbolism, and to contend that the Seljuks used the three colours which still retained a political significance in the Islamic world—blue, white and black—to epitomize their own importance. It may have been Byzantine influence which later led them to use pink as a form of the imperial purple, and the influence of the Chinese regard for yellow which resulted in their inclusion of yellow and gold.

The best of the Seljukid tiles are in no way inferior to the finest produced by other civilizations, but even more accomplished are the tile mosaics and ceramic inscriptions fashioned by their potters. In order to make a tile mosaic glazed panels had to be cut into various shapes which were then fitted neatly together. The task became still more complicated when an inscription was required for then the letters had either to be carved out of a glazed panel and stuck to a coloured background, or else cut into the panel while it was still damp and then glazed and fired.

The skill required for the production of these panels found fullest expression in the tiles which were intended as adornments for the royal palaces. Many of these were star-shaped, which necessitated a slight curving of one side of the tile and the cutting away of the corresponding side of the adjoining tile so that a close fit could be achieved. They displayed a glowing variety of colours in which gold played an important part. Their decorations, executed prior to glazing, included arabesques or variations of the arabesque derived from triangular or other geometric shapes, the corners of which had been rounded off. Small spaces at the centres of these designs were filled in with

Fig. 53
Plate 69

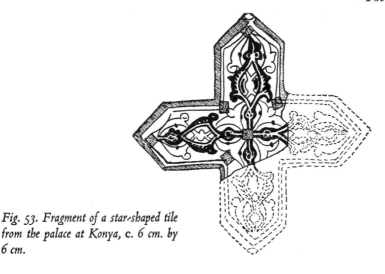

Fig. 53. Fragment of a star-shaped tile from the palace at Konya, c. 6 cm. by 6 cm.

a human figure or a flower. The drawing is invariably firm yet delicate.

It is unfortunate that only one painting of the Seljukid period is known to us; it appears on the inner faces of a Koran stand which was presented in 1278 to Celaleddin Rumi by Cemal-eddin Sahibi. Though it is badly worn, enough survives of the floral scrolls, eagles and lions forming the design to link the style to the painted decorations of the Capella Palatina at Palermo, and thus to indicate what the painted decorations of Konya's Kiosk must have been like.

PAINTING
Plates 72, 73

Plate 72

If we know little about the painting, the gap in our know-ledge is even greater with regard to the range and quality of the precious objects with which the wealthy Seljuks liked to sur-round themselves, for practically everything of value has perished. In about the year 1200 the Ortokid ruler is known to have possessed a remarkable water clock which was constructed for him by the great mechanic Djaziri,[90] but although there is every likelihood that the Seljukid sovereign owned objects as rare and as up-to-date as the clock, none has survived.

METAL-
WORK

Plates 42, 48

Plate 64

Plate 47

Plate 48

Plate 65

From Orkhon times down to the present day the Turks have always distinguished themselves by their skill in working metals, yet very few examples of Seljukid metalwork have come down to us, and none of those that survives is of the highest quality. The only piece of importance, in so far as Asia Minor is concerned, is an enamel and bronze dish which was made for the Ortokid ruler Sukman during the first half of the 12th century. The dish is now preserved at Innsbruck; both its shape and its enamel decorations reflect strong Byzantine influence together with more than a trace of the Persian style. More characteristic are the weights, of which a bronze example in the Bibliothèque Nationale in Paris is to be noted. A Seljukid weight of the same type in the Koyunoglu collection is much clumsier, but a gold buckle belonging to the Berlin Museum is well designed and skilfully executed; its style is closer to that of Caucasian sculpture than to the Ortokid bronzes or to Persian jewellery, yet it is sufficiently akin to some of the Anatolian carved stone work to justify its assignation to Asia Minor.

TEXTILES

Plate 77

The very few fragments of Seljukid silk brocades which exist are of the highest order. In their day they were widely admired and much sought after. Though an ambiguously-worded pas- sage in Marco Polo's *Travels*[91] seems to imply that they, and also Seljukid carpets, were made by Christian workers, and although it is very likely that Christians were employed side by side with Muslims in the workshops, it is nevertheless impos- sible to ascribe the cartoons of the surviving brocades to other than Islamic designers. The splendid fragment preserved in the Musée des Tissus at Lyons actually bears the name of Alaeddin Keykûbad woven into its border. Its design is typically Seljukid. Equally superb and no less characteristic is another brocade, two pieces of which survive in Germany; on these the central design consists of a double-headed eagle enclosed in a heart-shaped lozenge similar to that which appears on the Kayseri bowl. Though this shape is generally associated with the shield of Western heraldry it is also one which figures in Islamic heraldry, where it probably represented a badge of office, the meaning of which has now been forgotten.[92]

Plate 78

Plate 74

Though the border is missing from these fragments, with the result that neither is inscribed, there can be little doubt that they were woven in Anatolia for a royal patron; it is indeed tempting to assign both to a royal workshop. Figured silks such as these are extremely rare, but one of the earliest entries in the inventory recording the gifts presented to the Sultans of the Ottoman dynasty concerns a robe which Keyhüsrev III sent to Osman Bey;[93] it is described as a short-sleeved garment made of Denizli cloth woven with a crescent design. The robe has not survived, and the garments which belonged to Celaleddin Rumi's son, the Sultan Walad, and are now exhibited in the Mevlana Museum at Konya, are for the most part either of watered silks or of striped or checked stuffs.

Seljukid carpets were renowned in their day, and the suggestion that they were made by Christians is unconvincing, as rugmaking has always been a nomadic craft; even the Byzantines, though they excelled at most crafts, do not seem ever to have practised it. A specific group of carpets is now associated with the Seljuks, the rugs belonging to it being known as Konya carpets. The group comprises eight rugs which formerly belonged to the Alaeddin Mosque at Konya and three from the Eşrefoglu Mosque at Beyşehir the importance of which was not recognized till 1905. They are now in the Mevlana Museum at Konya. The Museum of Turkish and Islamic Art in Istanbul also owns some examples of the same type; some others which, though purchased in Egypt, are of Anatolian

Plates 70, 76

origin are now preserved in Sweden. All are made of two-ply wool with knotting of the Ghiordes type, amounting to eighty-three knots to the square inch. The prevailing colours in these carpets are a pale and dark brown, an ochre, a pale and dark red, a light and dark blue, purple and green; the basic design takes the form of an unfinished interlace.[94] Two of those from the Alaeddin Mosque are so large that Erdmann[95] thinks that they must have required special looms, and this leads him to conclude that they were made in a royal workshop.

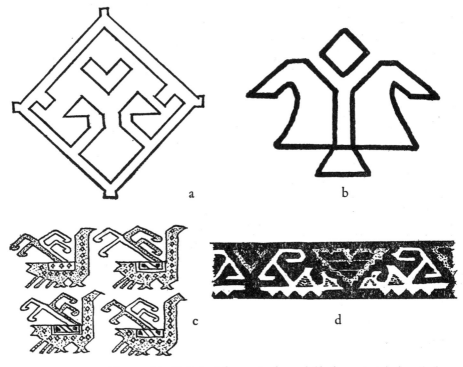

a   b

c   d

Fig. 54. Motifs derived from animals, probably horses, set back to back. a. from a carpet from the Alaeddin Mosque, Konya (see plate 76); b. from a Konya carpet excavated in Egypt; c and d. from two rugs from the Alaeddin Mosque, Konya.

Many of the rugs have star and rosette motifs which vividly recall certain of the appliqué felt hangings from Pazirik;[96] other patterns can be traced back to bird, animal or human forms;[97] on others again the Kufic lettering forming the borders is so strongly stylized as to have become illegible; at the same time it has acquired a resemblance to some of the devices which figure in Altaian art. Other shapes appear to stem from the brand marks which the earlier nomads used on their cattle and the later Ghuzz on their possessions, recalling in their turn the

Plate 70

Fig. 54

Figs. 55a to c

Fig. 56

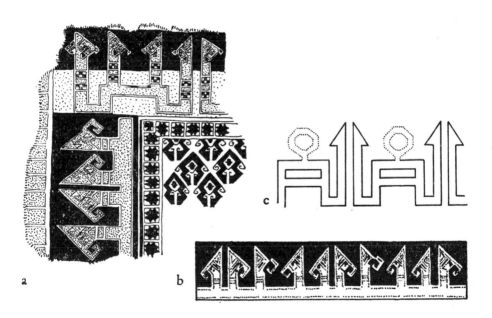

Fig. 55. a. Section of an almost complete rug from the Alaeddin Mosque, Konya. Width c. 3 m. (see also plate 76); b. a detail of the same rug's border showing its exaggeratedly-stylized Kufic motif; c. border of over-stylized Kufic lettering from a 13th-century Konya carpet found at Fostar.

gul or distinctive triangular mark of the more modern Turcomans. Artin Pacha[98] noted that Central Asian women of his
own day still continued to weave into their rugs the brand
marks which their husbands applied to their animals, and it
may well be that ancient cyphers of this type were introduced
into Asia Minor by nomads and transmitted in this manner to
craftsmen, who continued to use in their carpets shapes of
which they had forgotten the meaning.

Figs. 57, 58

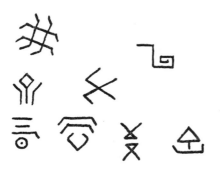

Fig. 56. Some 20th-century Central-
Asian brand marks, the designs of
which appear in Seljukid carpets, as,
for example, in Figures 54 and 55.

Fig. 57. Detail from a Konya type of
rug now preserved in Sweden.

Time has dealt harshly with Seljukid art in Asia Minor. Though a good many monuments have survived, the majority are much damaged; of the minor works practically everything has disappeared; yet, in each case, the little that exists suffices to reverse completely the judgement of those 19th-century scholars who regarded the Seljuks as a group of barbarians lacking in constructive ability and in artistic talent. Thus, whenever we pause once again to reflect on the tumultuous events of their short history, to assess their achievements in the administrative sphere, to gaze upon their works of art and to study their literature, it becomes a matter of astonishment that so relatively small a group of nomads contrived in the space of some two centuries to carve a kingdom for themselves out of the territories of infinitely larger states, to endow it with a distinctive culture of its own and to inspire its people with a sense of nationhood which enabled them to emerge from the Mongol occupation with their spirit unbroken. During their relatively short existence the Seljuks' remarkable energy played a vital part in transforming the Middle Ages of the Islamic world into an exciting and truly significant period in the history of Muslim art and culture.

Fig. 58. A fragment from a large carpet from the Alaeddin Mosque, Konya.

Notes

CHAPTER I

[1] M. A. Czaplicha, *The Turks of Central Asia* (Oxford, 1918), pp. 60–3.

[2] M. Defrémery, 'Histoire des Seldjoukides', *Journal Asiatique* (January 1848), vol. 2, p. 241.

[3] V. Barthold-Gibb, *Turkestan down to the Mongol Invasion* (E. J. W. Gibb Memorial Series, 1928), p. 287; and V. Barthold, *Histoire des Turcs d'Asie Centrale* (1945), chap. 8, p. 42.

[4] D. M. Dunlop, *The History of the Jewish Khazars* (Princeton, 1954), pp. 258–261.

[5] Barthold-Gibb, *op. cit.*, p. 10.

[6] See Appendix II A.

[7] Dunlop, *op. cit.*, pp. 258–61.

[8] Barthold, *op. cit.*, pp. 10–39.

[9] Barthold-Gibb, *op. cit.*, p. 237.

[10] Barthold-Gibb, *op. cit.*, p. 308.

[11] V. Bartold, *Khalif i sultan* (St Petersburg, 1912).

[12] W. E. D. Allen, *History of the Georgian People* (London, 1932), p. 87.

[13] S. Runciman, *History of the Crusades*, vol. I (Cambridge, 1951), p. 68.

[14] Runciman, *op. cit.*, vol. I, pp. 62–3.

CHAPTER II

[15] Anna Comnena, *The Alexiad*, translated by E. Dawes (London, 1926), p. 398.

[16] Anna Comnena, *op. cit.*, p. 152.

[17] Anna Comnena, *op. cit.*, p. 153.

[18] René Grousset, *Histoire des Croisades et du Royaume Franc de Jérusalem* (Paris, 1934), vol. 1, p. 29; and Runciman, *op. cit.*, vol. 2, pp. 170–80.

[19] Anna Comnena, *op. cit.*, p. 360.

[20] Anna Comnena, *op. cit.*, p. 397.

[21] S. Runciman, *op. cit.*, vol. I, p. 111.

[22] P. Wittek, 'L'Epitaphe d'un Comnène à Konya', *Byzantion*, X, p. 508.

[23] W. Heyd, *Histoire du Commerce du Levant au Moyen Age* (Leipzig, 1936), vol. 1, p. 303.

[24] C. Huart, *Konya, ville des Derviches Tourneurs* (Paris, 1897), p. 144.

[25] See Appendix II B.

[26] V. Gordlevsky, *Gosudarstvo Seldjukidov Maloi Azii* (USSR Academy or Science, 1941), pp. 30–7.

[27] Gordlevsky, *op. cit.*, p. 37.

[28] P. Wittek, 'Yasijioglu 'Ali on the Christian Turks of the Dobrudja', *BSOAS* (1952).

[29] Wittek, *op. cit.*, pp. 659–60.

[30] Deno J. Geanokoplos, *The Emperor Michael Paleologos and the West* (Harvard, 1959), pp. 29, 181.

[31] Wittck, *op. cit.*, p. 648.

[32] J. Laurent, 'Byzance et les origines du Sultanat de Roum', *Mélanges Diehl*, vol. 1 (Paris, 1930).

[33] Heyd, *op. cit.*, vol. 2, p. 162.

[34] Wittek, *op. cit.*, p. 649.

[35] Yacub Artin Pacha, *Contribution à l'étude du blazon en Orient* (London, 1902), p. 149.

[36] Tahsin Oz, *Turkish Textiles and Velvets* (Ankara, 1950), pp. 14–15.

CHAPTER III

[37] Barthold, *op. cit.*, p. 10.

[38] Fuad Köprülü, 'Türk edebiyatinin Mensai' *Milli tetebbüler mecmuasi*, no. 4 (Istanbul, 1926).

[39] Gordlevsky, *op. cit.*, p. 167.

[40] Cl. Huart, 'Epigraphie Arabe d'Asie Mineure', *Revue Sémitique* (Paris, 1894), p. 79.

[41] Gibb-Barthold, *op. cit.*, p. 305.

[42] Fuad Köprülü, *op. cit.*

[43] F. Sarre, *Reise in Kleinasien* (Leipzig, 1894), pp. 24–5.

[44] Anna Comnena, *op. cit.*, p. 165.

[45] Yacub Artin Pacha, *op. cit.*, p. 62, and S. Lane Poole, *Catalogue of the Oriental Coins in the British Museum*, vol. 8 (1877).

[46] Yacub Artin Pacha, *op. cit.*, p. 32.

[47] Huart, *op. cit.*, p. 325.

[48] V. Barthold, *K voprosu o pogrebalnom obriade turok i mongolov*, p. 65.

[49] Barthold, *loc. cit.*

[50] T. Talbot Rice, *The Scythians* (London, 1956), p. 114.

[51] Raymond Cox, *Les soieries d'art depuis les origines à nos jours* (Paris, 1914), p. 83.

[52] A. S. Unver, *La première école de médecine turque*, p. 8.

[53] A. S. Unver, *Une étude et quelques légendes sur les stations balnéaires d'Anatolie aux temps des Seldjoukides et dans les périodes suivantes.*

[54] Heyd, *op. cit.*, vol. I, p. 112.

[55] Heyd, *op. cit.*, vol. I, p. 302.

[56] A. Papadopulos-Kerameus, *Fontes Historiae Imperii Trapezuntiai* (1897), vol. I, p. 117.

[57] *The Journal of Friar Rubruquis* (Hackluyt Society, 1902), p. 184.

[58] Heyd, *op. cit.*, vol. I, p. 298.

[59] Seton Lloyd and Storm Rice, *Alanya* (Ala'iyya), (London, 1958).

[60] Huart, *op. cit.*, p. 370.

[61] Heyd, *op. cit.*, vol. I, p. 554.

[62] Heyd, *op. cit.*, vol. I, p. 21.

[63] See S. Lane Poole, *Vol. 8. Catalogue of Oriental Coins in the British Museum*, no. 194, p. 77.

[64] Gibb-Barthold, *op. cit.*, p. 310.

CHAPTER IV

[65] Fuad Köprülü, *Encyclopaedia of Islam*, Article on the Turkish language.

CHAPTER V

[66] Creswell, *A Short Account of Early Muslim Architecture* (London), pp. 9, 15–16, 80.

[67] A. Gabriel, *Monuments Turcs d'Anatolie* (Paris, 1934), p. 34.

[68] Behçet Unsal, *Turkish Islamic Architecture* (London, 1959), p. 17.

[69] G. Bell, *Amurath to Amurath* (London, 1924), p. 353.

[70] Rubruquis, *Travels in Tartary and China in 1253*, translated by de Bergeron (The Hague, 1735), chap. 2, p. 6; drawings on pp. 7 and 8.

[71] Strelkoff, *Survey of Persian Art*, vol. I (Oxford, 1931), pp. 450–2, dates these ossuaries to the 1st century A.D., but the staff of the Hermitage Museum at Leningrad now considers that none is earlier than the 5th century A.D.

[72] Creswell, *op. cit.*, p. 9.

[73] For a detailed study see Seton Lloyd and D. Storm Rice, *Alanya* (Ala'iyya) (The British Institute of Archaeology at Ankara, London, 1958).

[74] A. L. Mongait, *Arkeologia CCLP* (Moscow, 1955), p. 286.

[75] L. Laborde, *Voyage en Asie Mineure* (Paris, 1838).

[76] Ch. Texier, *Asie Mineure* (Paris, 1862).

[77] C. Huart, 'Epigraphie Arabe d'Asie Mineure', *Revue Sémitique* (Paris, 1894), pp. 151–65.

[78] F. Sarre, *Der Kiosk von Konya* (Berlin, 1931), and also by the same author, *Reise in Kleinasien* (Berlin, 1896).

[79] From Gibb-Barthold, *op. cit.*

[80] T. Talbot Rice, *The Scythians* (London, 1957), pp. 61, 140–2, 156 and 161.

[81] Niko Tchubinashvili, *Gruzinskaya rezba po derevu* (Tbilisi (Tiflis), 1958).

[82] Artin Pacha, *Contribution à l'étude du blazon en Orient* (London, 1902), p. 43.

[83] J. Strzygowski, 'Eléments asiatiques dans l'art', *Revue des Arts Asiatiques* (Annales du Musée Guimet), vol. 6, no. I, p. 27; and *op. cit.*, p. 9.

[84] T. Talbot Rice, *op. cit.*, plate 5.

[85] T. Talbot Rice, *op. cit.*, figs 57, 58 and 60 are but a few examples from many.

[86] T. Talbot Rice, *op. cit.*, plates 35 and 44.

[87] E. Kühnel, 'Der Lautenspieler in der islamischen Kunst des 8 bis 13 Jahrhunderts', *Berliner Museum Berichte* (new series, 1951), vols 3 and 4, pp. 29–35.

[88] F. Sarre, *Seldjukische Kleinkunst* (Leipzig, 1909), plate 3, and *Bir Selçuk Kabartmasi* (Istanbul, 1936).

[89] Artin Pacha, *op. cit.*, pp. 18–42.

[90] H. W. Haussig, *Kulturgeschichte von Byzanz* (Stuttgart, 1959), p. 253.

[91] Marco Polo, *Travels* (Penguin Classic), p. 16.

[92] L. A. Mayer, *Saracenic Heraldry* (Oxford, 1932), pp. 8, 19; figs 33, 34.

[93] Tahsin Oz, *Turkish Textiles and Velvets* (Ankara, 1950), pp. 14–15.

[94] C. J. Lamm, 'The Marby rug and some fragments of carpets found in Egypt', *Svenska Orientsållskapets ärsbök* (Stockholm, 1937), pp. 52–130.

[95] K. Erdmann, *Der Türkische Teppich des 15 Jahrhunderts* (Istanbul).

[96] T. Talbot Rice, *loc. cit.*

[97] See *Türk Etnografya Dergisi* (Ankara, 1956), plate XLIII.

[98] Artin Pacha, *op. cit.*, pp. 188–90, fig. XX.

Sunis, Shi'ites, Ismailis and Assassins

Towards the middle of the 8th century A.D. the collapse of the Ummayad dynasty and the ascendancy of that of the Abbasids led to much unrest among Muslims. Many became schismatics, others encouraged the growth of various religious sects and, before long, the bulk of the Muslim people split into two equally devout and almost equally powerful groups. The larger group comprised the orthodox Muslim supporters of the Abbasid caliphs of Baghdad; they called themselves Sunis, taking their name from the Arabic word *suna*, meaning 'the orthodox tradition or creed', because it expressed their conviction that the register or Suna of Muhammad's deeds, words and opinions, together with certain axioms propounded by the first Imams, alone represented the whole of the Prophet's teaching. As such they looked upon the Suna as distinct though complementary to the Koran, which they considered to have been entirely inspired by Allah.

The second faction was that of the Shi'ites; they were less dogmatic in their outlook, but they were opposed to the Abbasids, favouring the claim made to the Caliphate by the Fatimids of Egypt. The Fatimids were Shi'as who proclaimed their devotion to Fatima, the Prophet's favourite daughter and the wife of his beloved disciple Ali, by calling themselves after her. The bulk of the Persian Muslims were also Shi'ites and so too, in the 10th and 11th centuries, were the Buyids of Horasan, an autocratic Iranian dynasty tracing its descent back to the legendary hero Bahram Gur.

In the 11th century the Fatimids became the protectors of a Shi'ite sect known as the Ismaili. Among their new converts was a Persian Shi'ite who claimed to be a native of Tus, though he in fact came from Horasan. His name, Hasan-as-Sabbah, was destined to survive in history, for, although there is no truth in the story which describes the Nizam al Mulk,

Omar Khayyam and Hasan-as-Sabbah as contemporaries and fellow-schoolboys, he did in fact become Chamberlain to Alp Arslan. The role which he played in the latter part of his life was, however, more important than that which he filled as a courtier.

On becoming an Ismaili, Hasan withdrew from the capital to establish himself in the virtually impregnable fortress of Qasir Rud, better known to the West as Alamut or 'The Eagle's Nest'. It stood on the summit of a great peak in Horasan, somewhat to the north of Kazvin and south of the Caspian Sea. There Hasan founded an erotic, fanatical and politically-minded brotherhood of which he became the Grand Master. Its purpose was to bring about the downfall of the Abbasids by means of political murder and to raise the Fatimids to the Caliphate. Members of the sect were known as the Hashishiyun or Hashish Smokers, because one of the founder members, Abdul Malik ibn Tutaç, was a doctor who was well-versed in the use of hashish. He administered the drug to the brothers forming the highest grade in the hierarchy, who were known as the Companions of the Grand Master, but forbade it to the lower rank, that of the Destroying Angels, because of the lethargy which it induces. It was the duty of the Destroying Angels to carry out the political murders demanded by the Grand Master; they did so with the utmost daring, often warning their intended victim and trying to kill him in public, even though they thereby risked almost certain death at the hands of an infuriated crowd. Those who escaped with their lives returned to Alamut, where promotion and the joys of hashish-smoking awaited them. It was thus that the languages of Europe became enriched by the addition to their vocabularies of the word 'assassin', a perversion of Hashishiyun, and that many dire and ignoble pages were added to the history of the Muhammadan religion.

A. *The Samanids and the Ghaznavids*

The Samanids, like the Caliph's vizirs, the Barmecides, came from Balk and were probably of Iranian stock, though some authorities think that they may have been of Tadjik origin. In the 10th century they ruled over Horasan, a district which, with Buhara as its capital, then comprised much of Central Asia, in addition to northern Persia and Herat. The Samanids were Sunis and as such vassals of the Abbasids. In the 10th century their power began to decline in the face of Ghuzz pressure on their borders and because they began to allow the Ghuzz to find employment in their army as mercenaries.

Among the slaves employed by Malık Shah of Saman was a Ghuzz called Sabuktegin. He was able to render signal service to his master, who rewarded him in the year 961 with the governorship of Horasan. Within three years, in disregard of his oath of loyalty, Sabuktegin had established himself as the ruler of a state having Ghazna as its capital. Ghazna lay in Afghanistan, a hundred miles or so south-west of Kabul, straddling the main caravan road from Persia to the Ganges. Through it the new kingdom became linked to India, but its ruler was a Suni, who, by pledging his support to the Abbasid caliphs, automatically became concerned with political events in Baghdad.

B. *The Kingdom of Kwarazm*

The Ghuzz official Bilgetegin had a slave called Anuştegin, whom he took with him when he went to Merv to serve the Samanid ruler Malık Shah. Before long Anuştegin contrived to get himself appointed Superintendent of the Royal Washing Utensils. This was a valuable sinecure, for the department was run on the revenues derived from Kwarazm, with the result that the official in charge of it automatically became governor of Kwarazm. During the opening centuries of the present era Kwarazm had been a flourishing and independent kingdom.

It was among the first to become converted to Islam and this led the Kwarazmians to adopt a number of Persian customs and conventions while at the same time, under Ghuzz pressure, they gradually became Turkisized. Eventually they found themselves reduced to acknowledging the Samanid rulers as their suzerains. In 1097 an unsuccessful rebellion led the Samanid ruler to despatch Anuştegin's son to Kwarazm to restore order; the governor carried out his duties loyally and efficiently, devoting his leisure to acting as a patron of the arts. At his death in 1127 he was succeeded in office by his son Atzis, who assumed full sovereignty, annexing Djand and also some grazing land on the lower Syr Darya. A nomad revolt in that area provided Sencer with an excuse for despatching a punitive expedition against Kwarazm. On 15th November the Seljuks emerged victorious from a decisive battle, and although Atzis was able to escape with his life the Seljukid Sultan appointed his nephew Süleyman governor of Kwarazm. Some months later Atzis contrived to overthrow Süleyman, who fled to Sencer's court; soon after, another tribal revolt again brought the Seljuks into Transoxiana, but this time Atzis succeeded in defeating and evicting them from his kingdom.

In 1152 Atzis set out to reconquer Djand. By 1156 he had practically completed the task of regaining his former kingdom, but then, at the age of fifty-nine, he was struck with paralysis. Death followed quickly, but he had already re-established the independence of Kwarazm and founded a dynasty of considerable strength. He was succeeded by his son Arslan who devoted so much of his attention to increasing the army and attracting men of promise to it that he soon became the most powerful ruler in the eastern region of the Muslim world. His son and successor Takaş recaptured Herat, and Kwarazm endured as a powerful and independent state till its destruction by the Seljuks of Rum in 1232. Soon after, the Mongol invasion put an end to both the dynasties.

Buildings containing Particularly Fine Glazed Tile Work

Akşehir. Seyit Mahmut Hayrani's kümbet, 1237.

Amasya. The türbe in the Burmalı Cami, 1237–47.

Ankara. The mihrab in the Arslanhane mosque, a fine example of the baroque style executed in stucco and tile work, 1289.

Beyşehir. The Eşrefoglu Cami, 1296. Tiles from the ruins of the royal palace which stood here are now exhibited in the Karatay Museum, Konya.

Birgi. The Ulu Cami, 1312.

Çay. Medrese, 1258.

Erzurum. Çifte Minareli Medrese, 1253.

Kayseri. Gülük Cami's mihrab, 1210.

Konya. Kılıçarslan II Mausoleum. The mihrab in the Alaeddin Cami. Sırçalı Medrese, 1242/43. Büyük Karatay Medrese, 1251. The Sahip Ata or Larende Cami, 1258/59. Ince Minareli portal, 1271. Tiles from Konya's kiosk are exhibited in the Karatay Museum, Konya.

Malatya. Ulu Cami, 1237.

Sivas. The royal mausoleum in the Daruşşifa Hospital, 1217. Gök Medrese, 1271.

Soke. Menteşoglu Süleyman Bey Cami, 1299.

Tokat. Gök Medrese, 1270.

Tentative Chronological Classification of the Seljukid Buildings in Asia Minor

AD	H		
1030	426	*Mayyafarıkın*	The Ulu Cami; restored in 1152–57.
1063	458	*Diyarbakır*	The basalt bridge. The first Ulu Cami, a royal foundation ascribed to Malık Shah Ilaldı and his son Mahmut.
1122	516	*Mardin*	Niçmeddin Gazi Medrese.
1135–40	530–35	*Kayseri*	The Ulu Cami, a Danışmend foundation.

AD	H		
1145	540	*Niksar*	The Ulu Cami, a Danışmend foundation.
		Amasya	Kus bridge.
			Iltakin bridge.
			Maydan or Sultan bridge, founded by Hundi Hatun, daughter of Sultan Mesud I.
		Diyarbakır	The Maydan Gate.
		Pazarören	Melik Gazi's türbe, a Danışmend structure.
1145/46	541	*Amasya*	Halifet Gazi's türbe.
1147	542	*Mayyafarıkın*	The Ulu Cami, founded by Hadjmeddin Alpi b Timurtaş.
			Bridge over the Batman Su between Mayyafarıkın and Ahlat.
1154	549	*Erdbil*	Medrese, restored in 1232.
1156	551	*Aksaray*	The Alaeddin Cami, founded by Kılıçarslan I.
		Konya	Completion of the first Alaeddin Cami. Kılıçarslan's türbe built by Yusuf of Hoçan prior to 1192.
1157	552	*Niksar*	The Yagıbaşan Medrese, a Danışmend foundation.
1162	557	*Konya*	The Iplıkçi Cami, founded by the Vizir Abu Said Altınapa; completed either in 1182 or 1202.
1165/66	561	*Harput*	The Ulu Cami, an Ortokid foundation.
1167	563	*Diyarbakır*	The Ulu Badan tower erected by the Ortokid ruler Muhammad; restored in 1184.
1176	572	*Mardin*	The Ulu Cami Minare.
1179	575	*Erzurum*	The Ulu Cami, a Saltukid foundation.
1180/81	576	*Divriği*	The citadel and its mosque, founded by the Menguçek Emir Süleyman Shahanshah; the mosque was built by Hasan b Piruz of Maragha.
		Niksar	The Ulu Cami.
1183	579	*Diyarbakır*	The Urfa Gate.
1192	588	*Tercan*	Mama Hatun kümbet, built by Muffadul of Ahlat.
1193	589	*Diyarbakır*	Medrese, built by the architect Mesud and the master mason Cafar b Muhara of Aleppo.

AD	H		
1194	590	*Zindciniye*	Medrese, built by Isa abu Dırhan.
1195/96	592	*Divriği*	The türbes of the Emir Shahanshah, the Emir Kamareddin and that of Sitte Melik, the latter built by Bahram of . . .
?	?	*Van*	The Ulu Cami.
1196	593	*Sivas*	The Ulu Cami.
1197	594	*Ankara*	The Alaeddin Cami.
1199	596	*Mayyafarıkın*	The Minaret.

UNDATED BUILDINGS
OF THE 12TH CENTURY

		Tercan	Han.
		Mercan	Mama Hatun Bridge.
		Erzurum	The Mehdi Abbas kümbet, the Gümüşlü or Gazi Giyaseddin türbe, the Karanlık or Emir Sadreddin türbe and five others, as well as the mescit and the minaret within the citadel enclosure.
1200–04	597–601	*Dunyasır*	The Ulu Cami, built by the brothers Ortok and Yuluk Arslan.
1201	598		Altınapa Han on the Konya–Beyşehir Road; founded by the Vizir Şemseddin Altın Apa. Onü Han on the Konya–Beyşehir Road.
1202	599	*Kayseri*	Hoça Hasan Medrese and türbe, founded by the Vizir Altın Apa. The Kayseri–Kırşehir bridge over the Kızıl Irmak.
1203	600	*Mayyafarıkın*	Keykâvus Medrese and the fortifications for which Abu Bakr ibn Eyub—perhaps the father of Melike Adiliye of Kayseri—was responsible.
1204	601		Kızıl Oren Han on the Konya–Beyşehir Road.
1205	604	*Kayseri*	The Ulu Cami altered. Sultan Hamam, founded by Gevher Nesibi Hatun, daughter of Kılıçarslan II, and her türbe. The Sifaiye or Giyasiye Medreseleri, a medical school

AD	H		

and a hospital, the earliest dual establishment of this type, founded by Keyhüsrev I, possibly as early as 1192, though 1205 is the more likely date, in honour of his sister Gevher Nesibi Hatun, also known as Seljuka Hatun.

Gülük Cami, founded by Atzis Elti, also known as Princess Mahperi Hatun, a daughter of Mahmud b Yagıbaşan, wife of Keykûbad I and mother of Keyhüsrev II; dated by some to 1210.

Bor Sarı Cami.

| 1209 | 606 | *Afyon* | The Altıgöz Bridge, founded by Haci Mehmet b Ilyas. |

Boyalık Köy Kureis Baba Medrese and türbe.

| 1210 | 607 | *Konya* | Nizamiye Medrese. |

Dokuzun Han (Derbend) on the Konya–Afyon Road.

Evdir Han on the Antalya–Afyon Road, a royal foundation completed in 1219.

1212	610	*Kayseri*	Yogun Burç tower, completed in 1219, and some fortifications.
1213	611	*Konya*	Fortifications.
1215/16	613	*Eşab-i-Keif (Afsin)*	Rabat of the Emir Nüsreddin al din Hasan b Ibrahim.
1216	614	*Akşehir*	Taş Medrese, the main gate built by Ali b Husein Emirdad; completed in 1260 at the expense of Ali b Husein.

Sinop Fortifications built by Abu Ali al Kattani of Aleppo.

1217	615	*Sivas*	The Daruşşifa or Sifaiye Medrese and the türbe of Keykâvus I; the hospital remained in use till 1916; built by Ahmet abu Bakr and Ahmet b Bizl of Maranda.
1218	616	*Nigde*	The Müeddin Cami.
1219	617	*Konya*	The Alaeddin Cami rebuilt by Muhammad Kaulan of Damascus and the master mason, the atabeg Ayaz; completed in 1220/21.

Ferguniye Cami (a domed mosque).

AD	H		
		Antalya	Beşare Beg Mescid.
1220/21	618	*Konya*	City and citadel walls.
		Niksar	Kırk Kızlar kümbet.
		Kubadiye Palace	Completed in 1236.
		Sivas	Fortifications.
			Alay Han on the Aksaray–Kayseri Road; a royal foundation completed in 1225.
1223	620	*Diyarbakır*	The Mesud Medrese, founded by the Ortokid rulers Sukman I and Mesud.
		Nigde	The Alaeddin Cami, founded by Beşare b Abdulla and built by Sıddık and Gazi Mahmut.
			Kadın Han on the Konya–Afyon Road.
			Gelendost Han on the Antalya–Afyon Road.
1224	622	*Kayseri*	Üç Kale, some of the walls and the Ok Deposu.
		Amasya	The Emir Muharızaldın Halifa's türbe, built by al Kattani of Aleppo.
		Agros (Atabey)	Ertokus Medrese.
		Alaiye	Kızıl Kule and fortifications, built by al Kattani of Aleppo. Completed 1228.
1228	626		Çardak Han on the Burdur–Denizli Road.
1228/29	626	*Divriği*	The Ulu Cami and mental hospital.
1229	627		Sultan Han on the Konya–Aksaray Road; a royal foundation.
1230	628		Sultan Han on the Kayseri–Sivas Road, begun 1230.
			Alara Han on the Alaiye–Konya Road; a royal foundation.
		Konya	Hatuniye Cami.
			Şerafse Han on the Alaiye–Konya Road, completed in 1246.
			Kırkgöz Han and the bridge on the Antalya–Konya Road, completed in 1245.
			Süsüz Han on the Antalya–Konya Road.
			Obruk Han on the Konya–Afyon Road.
			Inçır Han on the Antalya–Afyon Road.
1232	630	*Eşab-i-Keif*	The mosque.

AD	H		
		Kastamonu	The medrese.
1233	631	Tokat	Türbe of Ebulkasim, son of the Vizir Ali al Tusi.
1234	632	Eşab-i-Keif	The han.
		Mardin	The Shahidiye Medrese begun, a royal foundation.
1234/35	633		Zazadin or Sadettin Han on the Konya–Aksaray Road, founded by Sadettin Köpek.
1235	633	Çankırı	Medrese of the Atabeg Cemaleddin Ferruk and his türbe.
		Kubadabad Palace	Built by Bedreddin Sutaş.
1236	634	Kayseri	Saraçeddin or Küçük Huand Medrese, founded by Saraçeddin Bada, Emir of Kayseri.
		Ilgın	Thermal Baths, perhaps built by Kaloyan of Konya.
1237/38	635	Kayseri	The Huand or Mahperi Hatun foundations, comprising a mosque, a hospital including the founder's türbe, and a bath, founded by the Princess of that name.
		Akşehir	Kümbet of the Seyit Hairani, built by Ahmet b Abdulla of Mosul.
		Amasya	Burmalı or Spiral Minaret, founded by Ferrukh, Master of the Hunt, and his brother, the treasurer Yusuf, perhaps built by Muhammad b Mahmut al Errani.
		Malatya	The Ulu Cami.
1238	636	Kayseri	Afghuniye Medrese. Sari Han, near Avanosa, on the Aksaray–Kayseri Road. Egridir Han on the Antalya–Afyon Road. Hatun Han on the Tokat–Pazar Road, founded by Princess Mahperi Hatun. Cimcimli Han on the Boyabat–Yeziköpü Road.
1239	637	Antalya	The Alaeddin Emir Mubarızeddin Armaganshah Medrese.
		Elbistan	The Ulu Cami. Çakallı Han on the Amasya–Havza–Kavak Road. Agzı Kara Han on the Aksaray–Kayseri Road; a royal foundation, begun 1231.

AD	H		
1240	638	*Kayseri*	Sıraçeddin Medrese founded by the Vizir Laleli Sıraçeddin.
		Amasya	Gök Medrese, completed in 1245, with its mosque and türbe.
		Divriği	The Kemankeş türbe.
			Karatay Han near Bunyan, on the Kayseri–Malatya Road; founded by the Vizir Celaleddin Karatay.
1241	639	*Erkilet*	Keyhüsrev's kiosk.
		Kayseri	Köşk kümbet.
1242/43	640	*Konya*	Sırçalı Medrese, a royal foundation, built by Muhammad of Tus and Bedreddin Muslıp.
		Egirdir	Medrese.
			Kargı Han on the Antalya–Adana Road.
1244	642	*Malatya*	The Musalla mihrab.
1246	644	*Kirşehir*	The Alaeddin Cami.
			Muzafereddin Muhammad's Medrese.
1247/48	645	*Kayseri*	The Sırçalı kümbet.
			Ali Cafar's kümbet.
			The türbe of Melike Adiliye Hatun, daughter of Melik al Adil abu Bakr Eyub, perhaps of Mayyafarıkın.
		Malatya	The Ulu Cami, a royal foundation. The dome was built by Abu Bakr of Malatya and the calligraphy was the work of his son Yakub and of Khusraw.
1248	646		Horozlu Han on the Konya–Ankara Road.
1249	647	*Kayseri*	Mosque and Medrese of Ebulkasim al Tusi (Haci Kiliç).
		Ankara	Fortifications restored.
			Işaklı Han. Built by Ali b Husein, whose türbe is in Tokat.
1250	648	*Tokat*	Bridge constructed for the Pervane Hamid im Ebulkasim, son of the Vizir al Tusi, and the Emir Seifeddaula.
		Antalya	Karatay Medrese, founded by the Vizir Celaleddin Karatay.

AD	H		
		Kirşehir	Türbe of the Mengüçek Prince Melik Gazi.
			Ak Han near Aksaray, founded by Seifeddin Kara- sungur, Emir of Ladık, completed in 1260.

Sometime between 1246–64, that is, in the reign of Kılıçarslan IV:

		Konya	The Kiosk.
1251	649	*Konya*	Büyük Karatay Medrese, founded by the Vizir Celaleddin Karatay.
		Tokat	Safer Pasha's türbe.
		Kayseri	Haidar Bey's Kiosk.
1253	651	*Erzurum*	Huand Hatun or Hatuniye or Çifte Medrese, founded by Huand Hatun.
1254	652	*Konya*	Küçük Karatay Medrese, founded by the Vizir Celaleddin Karatay.
1257	656	*Mardin*	Hatuniye Medrese.
1258	657	*Konya*	Ince Minareli Medrese founded by the Vizir Fakred- din Sahip Ata, built by Abdulla b Kelük. Malınçı Baba Medrese, built by Abdulla b Kelük. Larende or Energhe or Sahip Ata Cami, founded by the Vizir Sahip Ata and built by Abdulla b Kelük, Bey Hakim Cami.
		Çay	Medrese built by Galbek b Muhammad, founded by Emulbek ibn Muhammad.
1259	658	*Bursa*	Eski Kaplıça Hamam.
1262	661	*Sinop*	The Pervane Muin ed din Medrese.
1264	663	*Merzifon*	The Pervane Süleyman Muin ed din Cami.
1265	664	*Duragan*	Mosque and bath of the Pervane Muin ed din Süleyman.
		Develi	The Ulu Cami, a royal foundation.
		Konya	Mausoleum of Kılıçarslan IV's wife.
1267/68	667	*Kayseri*	The Sahibiye Medrese and fountain, founded by the Vizir Sahip Ata.
		Sinop	Mosque founded by the Pervane Süleyman Muin ed din.

AD	H		
1268	668		Kesik Köprü Han on the Kırşehir–Kayseri Road.
1269/70	670	*Tokat*	Gök Medrese, completed in 1271, used till 1811.
			Oresun Han on the Aksaray–Kayseri Road.
1271	671	*Sivas*	Gök Medrese founded by the Vizir Sahip Ata; tiles by Kaloyan of Konya.
			Bürüciye Medrese, founded by Muzaffer b Hibutalla of Barucird; possibly his own architect.
			Çifte Medrese founded by Şemseddin Juwaini, Grand Vizir of the Mongol Ilkhan of Persia.
1273	673	*Kastamonu*	The Ali b Pervane Medrese built by Sad of Kayseri.
		Afyon	The Ulu Cami, completed in 1277.
		Kırşehir	The Emir Nüreddin Civril Cacabey Medrese and türbe.
		Ahlat	Ulu türbe.
		Malatya	Ulu Cami restored.
1274/75	674	*Konya*	Sadreddin Konevi Cami and türbe.
		Ahlat	Hasan Padishah or Husain Aga b Mahmud's türbe.
1276	676	*Kayseri*	Shah Cıhan Hatun or Döner Kümbet.
		Amasya	Gök Medrese.
1277	677	*Konya*	Mausoleum of the Mawlana Celaleddin Rumi and his wife.
1278	678		Egret Han on the Konya–Afyon Road.
		Amasya	Sultan Mesud türbe.
			Çay Han on the Afyon–Kütahya Road.
1279	679	*Amasya*	Türbe of Seifeddin Turumtay, Emir of Amasya.
		Konya	Larende Cami hanıka, founded by the Vizir Sahip Ata.
		Ahlat	Iki türbe—Hasan Tımur Bugatay Aga and Şirin Hatun.
1282	682	*Konya*	Mausoleum of the Vizir Sahip Ata.
1287	687	*Tokat*	The Ahmet Pasha Cami founded by Idahund Hatun, daughter of the Pervane Süleyman Muin ed din, also her türbe.
1289	689	*Ankara*	The Ali Şerefeddin Arslanhane Cami.

AD	H		
1291	691	*Termen*	The Halef Gazi Cami founded by Haleb b Süleyman.
		Bitlis	The Ulu Cami.
		Tokat	Sünbül Baba Zazieysi or Halef Gazi Tekke, founded by Süleyman b Abdulla, freed man of the Princess Safvetaldın, daughter of the Pervane Muin ed din. Babşın Han on the Boyabat–Yeziköprü Road.
1296–98	696–98	*Beyşehir*	Eşrefoglu Cami.
1299	699	*Soke*	Menteşoglu Süleyman Bey Cami.
1301	701	*Beyşehir*	Türbe of Süleyman Eşrefoglu.
1302	702	*Nigde*	Türbe of Hawanda Hatun.
1308	708	*Amasya*	Tımurhan Medrese founded by Auben b Abdullak, slave of Ilduz Hatun.
1309	709	*Amasya*	Melike Hatun Bımarhane.
1312	712	*Nigde*	Türbe of Hudavend Hatun.
		Birgi	Ulu Cami.
1313	713	*Tokat*	Nüreddin ibn Sentimur türbe.

UNDATED BUILDINGS OF THE 13TH CENTURY

Artova Han	Gonçalı Han
Basara Han	Ibipsa Han
Çiflik Han	Kavak Han
Duragan Han	Tahtoba Han
Eli Kesik Han	Tol Han
Ezine Han	Pazar Han

CARAVANSERAIS

KONYA–AKSARAY ROAD
Zazadin or Sâdettin Han, founded by Sâdettin Köpek, 1234/35.
Obruk Han, 1230.
Sultan Han, a royal foundation, 1229.
Ak Han, 1250–60, founded by Seifeddin Karasungur, Emir of Ladik.*

KONYA–BEYŞEHIR ROAD
Altınapa Han, 1201.
Onü Han, 1201.
Kızıl Oren Han, 1204.

KONYA–ANKARA ROAD
Horozlu Han, 1248.

The Seljuks

ALTINAPA HAN–DERBEND ROAD
Eli Kesik Han.
Beşara Han.

KONYA–AFYON ROAD
Dokuzun Han, 1210.
Kadın Han, 1223.
Işaklı Han, 1249; built by Ali b Husein.*
Çay Han, 1278.*
Egret Han, 1278.*

KONYA–DOGANHISAR ROAD
Kavak Han.

KAYSERI–SIVAS ROAD
Sultan Han, often called Palaz Sultan
Han, 1230–36, a royal foundation.

AKSARAY–KAYSERI ROAD
Agzı Kara Han, begun by Keykûbad I
and completed by Keyhüsrev II, 1231–39.
Oresun Han, 1270.
Alay Han, 1220–25, a royal foundation.
Sarı Han, near Avanosa, 1238.

KIRŞEHIR–KAYSERI ROAD
Kesik Köprü Han, 1268.

KAYSERI–MALATYA ROAD
Karatay Han, 1240/41, founded by the
Vizir Celaleddin Karatay.

AFYON–KÜTAHYA ROAD
Egret Han, 1278.*
Çay Han, 1278.*

AFYON–AKŞEHIR ROAD
Işaklı Han, 1249.*

ALAIYE–KONYA ROAD
Şerafse Han, 1230.
Alara Han, 1230/31, a royal foundation.*
Kargı Han, 1242.*
Tol Han.

ANTALYA–AFYON ROAD
Evdir Han, 1210–19, a royal foundation.
Kırkgöz Han, 1230–45.
Süsüz Han, 1230.
Inçir Han, 1230.
Egridir Han, 1238.
Gelendost Han, 1223.
Ak Han, 1252–60.*

BURDUR–DENIZLI ROAD
Goncalı Han.
Çardak Han, 1228, founded by the Emir
Izzeddin Ayaz.

SIVAS–AMASYA ROAD
Yeni Han.
Artova Han.
Ibipsa Han.
Hatun Han, 1238, founded by Huand
Hatun.
Ezine Pazar Han.
Çiftlik Han.

ANTALYA–ADANA ROAD
Kargı Han, 1242.*
Alara Han, 1230/31.

YILDIZELI–TOKAT ROAD
Tahtoba Han.

AMASYA–HAVZA–KAVAK ROAD
Çakallı Han, 1239.

BOYABAT–YEZIKÖPRÜ ROAD
Duragan Han.
Tercan Han, c. 1200.
Eşab-i-Keif Han, 1234.
Cimcimli Han, 1238.
Babşın Han, north of Bitlis, 1291.

* Hans serving more than one trade route are distinguished by an asterisk.

BRIDGES

Diyarbakır, the basalt bridge, 1063.
Ahlat-Mayyafarıkın road bridge, 1147/48.
Bridge over the Kızıl Irmak on the Kayseri–Kırşehir road, *c.* 1200.
Tokat bridge, 1250.

KIOSKS

Unnamed kiosk on the Yosgad–Kayseri road, 1241.
Kayseri, the Haidar Bey Kiosk, 1251.

THERMAL BATHS AND SPRINGS

More than 200 have been recorded and the sites of 130 of these have been identified. The most important were those at:

Havza, where two baths were in use; the larger was founded by Mesud I in 1116 and was known both as the Sultan Mesud and the Sazı Pasha Bath; the smaller one was of much the same date; it was known as the Yüngüç Zade Mustafa Bath.

Kırşehir, where the Karakund Baths were three hours' travel from the town; they were founded in 1135 by Ali Karakund. His mausoleum stood close to them.

Ilgın, where the volcanic springs from which the town takes its name are two hours' travel from the city. The first bath built on the site was erected in 1236 by the Sultan Alaeddin Keykûbad I in gratitude for the curing of an attack of gout; it was rebuilt in 1267 by the Vizir Sahip Ata in the form of a double bath. The inscription which survives mentions Kaloyan as the builder, but it probably refers to the first structure.

Hamidiye, three-and-a-half hours' travel from the city, at a point close to the road leading to Konya.

Yoncal, on the Kütahya–Tursarlı road, 9 miles from Kütahya. Dated by an inscription to 1233. It was founded by Gülsün or Güsüm, daughter of the architect Ramazan.

SOME SELJUKID ARCHITECTS AND MASTER MASONS

Abu Bakr of . . . and Ahmet b Bizl, *doubtless the same as:*	Niksar, Kırk Kızlar kümbet, 1220.
Ahmet b Bakr and Ahmet b Bizl of Maranda.	Sivas, Sifaiye Medrese, 1217.
Abu Bakr and his son Yakub, both of Malatya.	Malatya, dome of the Ulu Cami, 1247.
Abu Ali b Ali-r-Rakka al Kattani of Aleppo.	Sinop, fortifications, 1216. Amasya, türbe of the Emir Muharızaldın, 1224. Alaiye, fortifications and the Kızıl Kule, 1224–28.
Ahmet b Ibrahim of Tiflis and Kuramshah of *Ahlat, son of Muhid of Ahlat.*	Divriği, the Ulu Cami and the mental hospital, 1228.

Ahmet b Abdulla of Mosul.	Akşehir, türbe of the Seyit Mahmut Hairani, 1237.
Ali b Husein Emirdad who, according to Huart, died in 1285.	Işaklı Han restorations, 1249. Akşehir, Taş Medrese, 1260.
Bahram of . . .	Divrik, türbe of Sitte Melik, 1195/96.
Bedreddin Sutaş, vali of . . .	Konya, Hatuniye Cami, 1230. Kubadabad Palace, 1235.
Galbek b Muhammad.	Çay, Medrese, 1258.
Hasan b Piruz of Maragha, master mason.	Divrik, Castle mosque, 1180/81.
Isa abu Dırhan.	Zindciniye Medrese, 1194.
Khusrau.	Malatya, the Ulu Cami, texts, 1247.
Kaloyan (interpreted by some as Kalo Yani, but could he perhaps be Keluk b Abdulla?) perhaps with Fahreddin Ali as his assistant.	Sivas, Gök Medrese, 1271. Sivas, Çifte Minareli ?, 1271. Ilgın, thermal baths, 1267.
Kelük or Mamlık b Abdulla, sometimes also called Kalus, and, thus, perhaps the same master as Kaloyn.	Konya, Sahib Ata Cami, 1258. Konya, Malınçı Baba Medrese, 1258. Konya, Ince Minareli Medrese, 1258. Sivas, Çifte Minareli, 1271.
Mesud, architect, and Cafar b Muhara of Aleppo, master mason.	Diyarbakır, Medrese, 1193.
Muhammad Kaulan of Damascus, architect, and Atabeg Ayaz, master mason.	Konya, final rebuilding of the Alaeddin Cami, 1219/20.
Muhammad or Osman Mehmet of Tus and Bedreddin Muslıp.	Konya, Sırçalı Medrese, 1242/43.
Muhammad b Mahmut al Errani (though perhaps a potter?).	Amasya, Burmalı Minare, 1237.
Muzaffer b Hibutalla al Barucı.	Sivas, Bürüciye Medrese, 1271.
Sad of Kayseri.	Kastamonu, Medrese, 1273.
Salı Mahmut, architect, and Yahya b Ibrahim, master mason.	Diyarbakır, Yedi Kardaş tower, 12th century.

Sesi Mufaddul, i.e. Mufaddul the Cross-eyed.	Tercan, Mama Hatun kümbet, 1192–1201.
The brothers Sıddık and Gazi b Mahmut.	Nigde, Alaeddin Cami, 1223.
Yusuf b Abdulgaffar of Hoçan.	Konya, Kılıçarslan's türbe, in the 1180's.
The brothers Yuluk and Ortok Arslan.	Dunyaşir, Ulu Cami, 1200–04.
The Pervane Hamid Ebulkasim, son of the Vizir al Tusi, with the son of Bahaeddin al Farac, known as ibn al-Hakim.	Tokat, the bridge, 1250.

WOODCARVERS

Haci Menguberti of Ahlat.	Ebony mimber in the Alaeddin Cami, Konya, 1145.
Ibrahim or Muhammad ibn Abu Bakr.	Mimber from Kızıl Bey Cami, Ankara, 1197.
Ahmet of Tiflis.	Mimber in the Ulu Cami, Divriği.
Omer ibn Iliyas of Karaman.	Doors of the Imaret Cami, Karaman.

CERAMICISTS

Ahmet ibn Bakr of Marand.	Sivas, Şifaiye Hospital, 1217. Niksar, Kırk Kızlar türbe, 1220.
Ahmet ibn Abdulla of Mosul.	Akşehir, türbe of the Seyit Mahmut Hairani, 1237.
Kerimeddin Erdınshah.	Konya, dome of the Alaeddin Cami, 1219–20.
Kaloyan of Konya.	Sivas, Gök Medrese, 1271.

CALLIGRAPHERS

Yakub ibn Yakub b Abu Bakr, builder of the Ulu Cami, Malatya.	Inscription in the Ulu Cami, Malatya, 1247.

O

Bibliography

ENGLISH

W. F. Ainsworth, *Travels and Researches in Asia Minor*, 1862.

W. E. D. Allen, *History of the Georgian People*, London, 1932.

T. Arnold, *Survivals of Sasanian and Manichaean Art in Persian Painting*, Oxford, 1924.

M. Bahrami, 'A gold medal in the Freer Gallery of Art', *Archaeologica Orientalia*, New York, 1952.

G. Bell, *Amurath to Amurath*, London, 1924.

H. Bowen, 'Notes on some Early Seljukid Vizirs', *British School of Oriental and African Studies*, no. XX, 1957.

E. G. Browne, *A Literary History of Persia*, London, 1931.

E. Cohn-Wiener, 'On the origin of the Persian carpet pattern', *Islamic Culture*, vol. XI, no. 4.

Anna Comnena, *The Alexiad*, E. Dawes's translation, London, 1926.

K. A. S. Creswell, *A Short Account of Early Muslim Architecture*. Pelican book, no. 407.

M. A. Czaplicha, *The Turks of Central Asia*, Oxford, 1918.

D. M. Dunlop, *The History of the Jewish Khazars*, Princeton, 1954.

Deno' J. Geanokoplos, *The Emperor Michael Paleologus and the West*, Harvard, 1959.

H. A. R. Gibb and W. Barthold, *Turkestan down to the Mongol Invasion*. E. J. W. Gibb Memorial Series; New Series; London, 1928.

R. Grousset, 'An outline of the history of Persia', *The Survey of Persian Art*, vol. I, Oxford, 1931.

P. W. Hasluck, 'Plato in the folklore of the Konya plain', *Annual of the British School at Athens*, no. XVIII.

—, *Christianity and Islam under the Sultans*, Oxford, 1921.

D. G. Hogarth, *A Wandering Scholar in the Levant*, London, 1899.

H. Hollis, 'A unique Seljuk bronze in the Cleveland Museum', *Ars Islamica*, no. 2.

C. J. Lamm, 'The Marby rug and some fragments of carpets found in Egypt', *Svenska Orientsållskapets årsbök*, 1937, pp. 52–130, Stockholm.

A. Lane, 'Ottoman Pottery of Isnık', *Ars Orientalis*, vol. II, Michigan, 1957, pp. 247–50.

S. LANE-POOLE, *Catalogue of the Oriental Coins in the British Museum,* vol. 8, 1877.

SETON LLOYD and D. STORM RICE, *Alanya* (Ala'iyya), London, 1958.

H. C. LUKASH, *The Fringe of the East,* London, 1913.

—, *The City of Dancing Dervishes,* London, 1914.

H. F. B. LYNCH, *Travels and Studies in Armenia,* London, 1901.

F. R. MARTIN, *History of Oriental Carpets before 1800,* Vienna, 1908.

SAMNULLAH MAWLAWI FADIL, *The Decline of the Saljukid Empire,* Calcutta, 1938.

L. A. MAYER, *Saracenic Heraldry,* Oxford, 1932.

V. MINORSKY, *Geographical Factors in Iranian Art,* London, 1938.

—, *Studies in Caucasian History,* London, 1953.

TAHSIN OZ, *Turkish Textiles and Velvets,* Ankara, 1950.

MARCO POLO, *Travels,* Penguin Classic.

A. U. POPE, *Masterpieces of Persian Art,* New York, 1945.

W. M. RAMSAY, *The Historical Geography of Asia Minor,* London, 1896.

R. M. RIEFSTAHL, *Turkish Architecture in South-Western Anatolia,* Harvard, 1931.

—, *The Art Bulletin,* no. XLIII, June 1931.

RUBRUQUIS, *Travels in Tartary and China in 1253,* in the Hackluyt Society edition and in that of de Bergeron, The Hague, 1735.

S. RUNCIMAN, *History of the Crusades,* vol. I, Cambridge, 1951.

T. TALBOT RICE, *The Scythians,* London, 1957.

H. F. TOZER, *Turkish Armenia,* London, 1883.

BEHÇET UNSAL, *Turkish Islamic Architecture,* London, 1959.

S. A. UNVER, *The Science of Medicine in the Seljuk Period,* Ankara, 1940.

P. WITTEK, 'Yasijioglu 'Ali on the Christian Turks of the Dobrudja', *BSOAS,* 1952.

—, 'The Rise of the Ottoman Empire', *Royal Asiatic Society Monograph,* no. 23, 1936.

KEMAL S. YETKIN, 'The Mausoleum of Mama Hatun', *The Burlington Magazine,* May 1957, pp. 146–7.

YAKUB ARTIN PACHA, *Contribution à l'étude du blazon en Orient,* London, 1902.   FRENCH

M. BAHRAMI, 'Le problème des ateliers d'étoiles de faiences lustrées', *Revue des Arts Asiatiques,* vol. X, no. 4.

V. V. BARTOLD, *Histoire des Turcs d'Asie Centrale*, Paris, 1945.

M. BROSSET, *Histoire de la Géorgie*, St Petersburg, 1849.

CL. CAHEN, 'Les Malik‑names et l'histoire des origines Seldjoukides', *Orient*, no. 2.

—, *Les Seldjouks de Rum*, Brussels, 1950.

R. COX, *Les soieries d'art depuis les origines à nos jours*, Paris, 1914.

M. DEFRÉMERY, 'Histoire des Seldjoukides', *Journal Asiatique*, January 1848, vol. 2.

—, 'Hamd Allah Mustaufi al Kazwini, Histoire des Seldjoukides et des Ismailiens ou Assassins de l'Iran, extraite du Tarikhi Guzideh ou Histoire Choisie de Mustaufi', *Journal Asiatique*, Paris, 1840, p. 142; also see *Journal Asiatique*, 1853, no. 5, and 1856, no. 13.

B. DENIKE, 'Quelques monuments de bois sculptés au Turkestan Occidental', *Ars Islamica II*, 1935.

M. DIEZ, 'Les monuments seldjoukides en Asie Mineure', *Bulletin de l'Art Ancien et Moderne*, August 1908.

A. GABRIEL, *Monuments Turcs d'Anatolie*, Paris, 1931.

—, *Monuments Turcs d'Anatolie*, Paris, 1934.

R. GROUSSET, *Histoire des Croisades et du Royaume Franc de Jérusalem*, Paris, 1934.

W. HEYD, *Histoire du Commerce du Levant au Moyen Age*, Leipzig, 1936.

TH. HOUTSMA, *Receuil de textes rélatifs à l'histoire des Seldjoukides*, vols 3 and 4, Leyden, 1886–1902.

CL. HUART, 'Epigraphie Arabe d'Asie Mineure', *Revue Sémitique*, Paris, 1894.

—, *Konya, ville des Derviches Tourneurs*, Paris, 1897.

L. LABORDE, *Voyage en Asie Mineure*, Paris, 1838.

J. LAURENT, 'Byzance et les origines du Sultanat de Roum', *Mélanges Diehl*, vol. I, Paris, 1930, pp. 177–82.

P. LEMERLE, *L'Emirat d'Aydin*, Presses Universitaires de France, Paris, 1957.

G. MARÇAIS, *Coupole et Plafond de la Grande Mosquée de Kairouan*, Paris‑Tunis, 1925.

G. MENDEL, 'Les monuments Seldjoukides d'Asie Mineure', *Bulletin de la Revue de l'Art Ancien et Moderne*, 1908.

G. MIGEON, *Manuel d'art Musulman*, Paris, 1927.

G. MIGEON, 'Notes d'archéologie Musulmane. A propos de nouvelles acquisitions du Louvre', *Gazette des Beaux Arts*, third series, vol. 33, 1905, p. 441.

V. P. MINORSKI, *Une nouvelle source musulmane sur l'Asie Centrale au XIme siècle*, Paris, 1937.

J. MOHLE, *Le Livre des Rois*, Paris, 1876–78.

R. MONTRAN, *Histoire de la Turquie*, Paris, 1952.

H. ROMASHEVITCH, 'Les sculptures de lions en Iran', *Arts et Archéologie Iraniens*, Moscow-Leningrad, 1939.

H. SALADIN, *Art Musulman*, Paris, 1906.

CH. SCHEFER, *Quelques chapitres de l'abrégé du Seljouk-nameh. Receuil de textes et traductions publiés par les professeurs de l'Ecole des langues orientales vivantes,* vol. I, Paris, 1889.

J. STRZYGOWSKI, *L'ancien art chrétien en Syrie*, Paris, 1936.

—, 'Les éléments asiatiques dans l'art', *Revue des Arts Asiatiques*, Annales du Musée Guimet, vol. 6, no. 1.

CH. TEXIER, *Asie Mineure*, Paris, 1862.

A. S. UNVER, *Hadji Pacha de Konya*.

—, *La première école de médecine et de clinique turque*, Istanbul, 1932.

—, *Une étude et quelques légendes sur les stations balnéaires d'Anatolie aux temps des Seldjoukides et dans les périodes suivantes.*

—, *Hippocrates et sa grande place dans la mythologie turque*, Paris, 1940.

M. VAN BERCHEM and HALIL EDHEM, *Matériaux pour un Corpus inscriptionum arabicarum. Troisième partie. Asie Mineure*, Cairo, 1910.

P. WITTEK, 'L'Epitaphe d'un Comnène à Konya', *Byzantion*, X.

—, 'Deux chapitres de l'histoire des Turcs de Roum', *Byzantion*, vol. XI.

GERMAN

W. BACHMANN, *Kirchen und Moscheen in Armenien und Kurdistan,* Leipzig, 1913.

W. BODE, *Vorderasiatische Knüpfteppiche*, Leipzig, 1901.

E. COHN-WIENER, *Turan, Islamische Baukunst in Mittelasien*, Berlin, 1930.

E. DIEZ and M. VAN BERCHEM, *Khurasanische Baudenkmäler*, Berlin, 1918.

E. DIEZ, *Persisch-Islamische Baukunst in Churusan*, Darmstadt-Gotha, 1923.

—, *Die Kunst Indiens*, Potsdam, 1925.

—, *Die Kunst der Islamischen Völker*, Berlin, 1935.

K. ERDMANN, *Der Türkische Teppich des 15 Jahrhunderts*, Istanbul.

K. ERDMANN, 'Nachträge zu den Beobachtungen einer Reise in Zentral-anatolien', *Jahrbuch des Deutschen Archäologischen Instituts.*

—, GLÜCK and E. DIEZ, *Die Kunst des Islam*, Berlin, 1925.

H. W. HAUSSIG, *Kulturgeschichte von Byzanz*, Stuttgart, 1959.

E. HONIGMAN, *Die Ostgrenze des Byzantinischen Reiches von 367–1070*, Brussels, 1927.

N. JORGA, *Geschichte des Osmanischen Reiches*, vol. I, Gotha, 1908.

E. KÜHNEL, 'Der Lautenspieler in der islamischen Kunst des 8 bis 13 Jahrhunderts', *Berlin Museum Berichte*, New Series, 1951, vols. 3 and 4.

—, *Islamische Kleinkunst*, Berlin, 1925.

C. PREUSSER, *Nordmes sopotamische Baudenkmäler Altchristlicher und Islam-ischer Zeit*, Leipzig, 1913.

F. SARRE, *Reise in Kleinasien*, Leipzig, 1894.

—, *Seldjukische Kleinkunst*, Leipzig, 1909.

—, *Kunst des alten Persien*, Berlin, 1922.

—, *Der Kiosk von Konya*, Berlin, 1931.

F. SARRE and M. VAN BERCHEM, 'Das Metalbecken des Atabeks Lulu von Mosul in der Bibliothek von München', *Münchener Jahrbuch der Bildenden Künste*, no. L, Halbband, 1907.

H. G. SCHMIDT, 'Persische Seidenstoffe der Seldjukerzeit', *Ars Islamica*, 1935.

J. STRZYGOWSKI and M. VAN BERCHEM, *Amida*, Heidelberg, 1910.

J. VON HAMMER, *Geschichte des Ottomanischen Reiches*, Budapest, 1827–1835.

P. WITTEK, *Das Fürstentum Mentesche*, Istanbul, 1934.

LATIN

A. PAPADOPULOS-KERAMEUS, *Fontes Historiae Imperii Trapezuntiae*, vol. I, 1897, St Petersburg.

TURKISH

CELAL ESAD ARSEVEN, *Türk Sanatı Tarihi*, Istanbul, vols I to 10.

O. ASLANAPA and E. DIEZ, *Türk Sanatı*, Istanbul, 1955.

Islam Ansiklopedisi, Istanbul, 1954, nos. 62 and 63.

MESUD KOMAN and S. ÜÇER, *Sırrı Konya Ili, koy ve yer adları üzerinde bir deneme*, Konya, 1945.

FUAD KÖPRÜLÜ, 'Türk edebiyatinin Mensai', *Milli tetebbüler mecmuası*, nos. 4 and 5, Istanbul, 1926.

—, 'Bizans müesseselerinin tesiri', *T.H.I.T.M.*, vol. I, 1931, pp. 165–313.

FUAD KÖPRÜLÜ, 'Oguz etnolojisine dair tarihi notlar', *Türkiyat mecmuası*, vol. 1.

KAZIM ÖZDOGAN, *Keyseri Tarihi*, vol. 1, Kayseri, 1948.

T. ÖZGÜÇ and M. AKOK, *Üç Selçuklu Abidesi*, Ankara, 1958.

—, *Sarıhan*, Ankara, 1956.

—, *Melik Gazi türbesi ve kalesi*, Ankara, 1950.

—, *Candaroglu Mehmet Bey Cami*, Ankara, 1956.

—, *Alayhan, Oresunhan ve Hizırilyas Köskü*, Ankara, 1957.

—, *Develi Abideleri*, Ankara, 1955.

—, *Afşin Yakınındaki Eşab-i-Keif Külliyesi*, Ankara, 1958.

F. SARRE, *Bir Selçuk Kabartmasi*. A Seljuk relief in the Ankara museum, Istanbul, 1936.

Türk Etnografya Dergisi, Ankara, 1956.

Türkiye Tarihi Anıtları, Ankara, 1946.

F. UGUR and M. KOMAN, *Selçuk Büyüklerinden Celalüddin Karatay*, Konya, 1940.

MÜLRIMIN HALIL YINANÇ, *Türkiye Tarihi Selçuklar Devri*, Istanbul, 1944.

V. BARTOLD, *Khalif i sultan*, St Petersburg, 1912.

—, 'K voprosu o pogrebalnom obriade turok i mongolov', *Z.V.O.R.A.O.*, 1917–20, pp. 55–77.

—, 'K istorii religioznich dvizjeni X veka, *Izvestia of the Russian Academy of Science.*

V. GORDLEVSKY, *Gosudarstvo Seldjukidov Maloi Azii*, USSR Academy of Science, 1941.

S. V. KISELEV, *Drevnyaya istoria ujnoi Sibiri*, Moscow, 1951.

A. L. MONGAIT, *Arkeologia SSSR*, Moscow, 1953.

I. A. ORBELI, 'Problema Seldjuskovo iskusstva', *Arts et Archéologie Iraniens*, Moscow, 1939.

S. I. RUDENKO and A. N. GLUKOV, *Mogilnik Kishirgi na Altaye. Materiali po etnografii*, Leningrad, 1923.

N. TCHUBINASHVILI, *Gruzinskaya srednevekovaya hudojestvennaya rezba po derevu*, Tbilisi (Tiflis), 1958.

N. A. USEINOV, *Pamiatniki Azerbeidzhanskovo iskusstva*, Moscow, 1951.

A. L. YACOBSON, *Ocherk istorii zodchestva Armenii V–VIII v.*, USSR, 1950.

A. L. YACOBSON, 'Rannesrednevekovie Khersona', *Materiali, no.* 17.

Z.V.O.R.A.O., *Zapiski Voztochnovo otdeleniya Russkovo arckeologicheskovo obchshestva.*

JOURNALS AND SURVEYS

Ars Islamica.

Art et Archéologie Iraniens, Moscow-Leningrad, 1939.

British School of Oriental and African Studies, Journal of (BSOAS).

Bulletin de l'Art Ancien et Moderne.

Byzantion.

Encyclopaedia of Islam.

Gazette des Beaux Arts.

Journal Asiatique.

Orient.

Revue des Arts Asiatiques.

Survey of Persian Art, vol. I, both of the text and the plates, Oxford, 1931.

SOURCES OF ILLUSTRATIONS

Acknowledgement is due to the undermentioned for the photographs used in the plates: Messrs Brown, Antiquarian Booksellers, Eton, 9; Professor Kurt Erdmann, 70, 76; Miss V. Gordon and the Courtauld Institute, London, 17, 18, 39, 52; Miss Josephine Powell, 12, 13, 14, 19, 20, 21, 22, 24, 25, 26; Professor Storm Rice, 6, 64; Mr David Wilson, 31, 43, 44, 45, 46; British Museum, London, 10, 79, 80; Bibliothèque Nationale, Paris, 47; Musée Historique des Tissus, Lyons, 77; Staatliche Museen, Berlin, 63, Ehemals Staatliche Museen, Berlin-Dahlem, 65, 78; The Turkish Press and Tourist Bureau, 29, 30, 69, 71, 72, 73; Bay Koyunoglu of Konya, 42, 48, 75.

Sources of the figures are as follows: Ethnographical Museum, Ankara, 4, 48; Professor Celal Esad Arseven, 8, 15; Professors Tahsin Ozgüc, and Mahmut Akok, 5, 18, 19; Museum of Turkish and Islamic Art, Istanbul, 45; Professor Oktay Aslanapa, 10, 12, 14, 16, 17, 25, 26; Konya Museums, 36, 37, 46, 47, 50, 51, 52, 53; Bay Koyunoglu of Konya, 3; Professor Kurt Erdmann, 54b, 55a, 58; Mr Seton Lloyd, 9, 20a, b; Messrs Quaritch, 56; Victoria and Albert Museum, London, 4, 38, 39, 40.

7

9

10

17

18

20

21

24

25

7

28

29

30

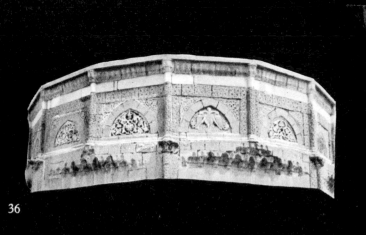

36

37

38

39

40

41

42

43

44

45

46

47

48

49

50

51

52

3

54

55

6

57

58

59

60

61

66

67

8

69

71

2

3

74

75

76

7

78

79

80

Notes on the Plates

1. The Hatuniye Cami, Konya, of which only the minaret has come down to us, was built in 1230 by Bedreddin Sutaş. It was probably as a result of this work that he was entrusted five years later with the construction of the royal palace of Kubadabad. He signed the Hatuniye Cami, adding the word *vali* after his name, but the name of the town of which he was mayor has disappeared from the inscription.

2. The Alaeddin Kiosk, Konya, as it appeared early in the present century. It was situated within the citadel walls, close to the Alaeddin Mosque, and when Texier visited Konya in the 19th century rather more of it was standing. Sarre, in his *Der Kiosk von Konya*, (Leipzig, 1936), provides convincing evidence for dating it to the reign of Kılıçarslan IV (1246–64). The kiosk was extensively decorated, sections being painted in a style which seems to have resembled that of the paintings in the Palazzo Reale at Palermo; and its walls were faced with glazed tiles of unusual shapes, colours and designs. Sculptured lions mounted guard over the kiosk and one was still in place when this photograph was taken.

3. The royal türbe or mausoleum built within the Alaeddin Cami, Konya, by Yusuf ibn Abdulgaffer of Hocan for Kılıçarslan II (1156–92) still contains the coffins of eight Seljukid sultans. Its severe lines and the absence of elaborate decoration are in accordance with its early date.

4. The Alaeddin Cami, Konya, which, standing with its mausoleum and palace within the walled citadel enclosure, formed the heart of the Sultanate. The mosque was begun by Sultan Mesud (1116–56) and completed by Keykûbad I in 1220/21. The latter employed Muhammad ibn Kaulan of Damascus as his architect and Syrian taste was responsible for the use of marble of two colours for its external decoration. Until 1905 the mosque retained eight of its original carpets. The ebony *mimber* or pulpit carved for it in 1145/46 by Haci Menguberti of Ahlat still remains in use, and its *mihrab* or altar is among the most beautiful of its period.

5. The ceiling in the dome of Büyük Karatay Medrese, Konya, rests on triangular pendentives, each of which is divided into five smaller triangular

P

sections. Both these and the dome itself are faced with glazed tiles of the finest quality; they represent the stars and the firmament in all their glory. An inscription in flowered Kufic, executed in glazed tile work, repeating the names of the first four caliphs, runs round the base of the dome; the triangular pendentives are adorned with geometric decorations. The prevailing colour is a deep blue, kindled by touches of gold; the general effect is light yet extremely grand.

6   The Büyük Karatay Medrese, Konya, founded by the Vizir Celaleddin Karatay in 1251, is now used to display the Mevlana Museum's collections of Seljukid ceramics and minor arts. The upper section of its portal is decorated in accordance with the Syrian taste, which dictated the external decorations of Konya's Alaeddin Cami some thirty years earlier, but the honeycomb stone work of the niche, the concentration of much of the ornament into panels and the use of pillasters of western origin reflect the taste of their own time.

7   Ince (or slender) Minare Medrese, Konya, so called because of its exceptionally high and slender minaret, was founded by the Vizir Fekreddin Sahip Ata and built by Keluk b Abdulla in 1258 to serve as a theological college. It now contains the Mevlana Museum's collection of Seljukid sculpture and ornamental plaster work. Its brick minaret was decorated with glazed bricks and tiles, but it was struck by lightning early in this century and destroyed. Much of the medrese was also built in brick, a rather unusual feature for the period, but its elaborately-sculptured portal is in stone.

8   Detail of the portal of Ince Minare Medrese, Konya. Its decoration depends to a large extent on the inscriptions, part of which take the form of two bands disposed in such a manner as to produce a ribbon-like effect. The rounded corners of the niche are filled in with floral ornaments of a baroque character. Indeed, like all Keluk's work, the conception of the decoration is essentially baroque, though it is subjected to such severity of treatment that it retains a classic imprint.

9   A drawing made in the year 1843 by the Hon. Robert Curzon of the the walls, minarets and turrets of Erzurum as seen from the window of the British Commissioner's house.

10 The walls of Konya's citadel as they appeared in 1825, a lithograph from L. de Laborde, *Voyage en Orient*, I, 1839.

11 Çifte (or double) Minareli Medrese, Sivas, founded in 1271 by the Vizir of the Mongol Ilkhan of Persia, Şemseddin Juwaini, is baroque in style. Compare the decoration of the upper section of the turret on the extreme left with that of its base, which is shown in greater detail on plate 13, whilst that of the turret on the far right is shown on plate 14.

12 Gök (or blue) Medrese, Sivas, derives its name from the blue tiles with which it was decorated. Founded by the Vizir Sahip Ata and built by Kelük b Abdulla in 1271/72, it is among the finest in Turkey. Many of the sculptures on its main façade resemble those of the somewhat earlier Laranda Cami, Konya, built by the same master. The door opens into a four-lobed vaulted hall, leading on the right into a small, domed mosque decorated with splendid tiles; beyond, a pool marks the centre of the courtyard. The lateral porticoes have central ivan-shaped halls flanked on either side by six rooms disposed on two floors.

13 The baroque trend which distinguished Seljukid decoration of the second half of the 13th century is clearly apparent in this detail of a capital from the Çifte Medrese, Sivas. In places the carving is as much as 16 cm. deep.

14 Another detail from the Çifte Medrese, Sivas, where interlinked bands similar in inspiration to those on Konya's Ince Minare Medrese (plate 8), built by the same master some twelve years earlier, form the basis of the design.

15 Portal of Sultan Han on the Konya–Aksaray Road, with a glimpse of the mosque beyond. This caravanserai was a royal foundation begun in 1229 and completed in 1236. Syrian influence is responsible for the lintel executed in two shades of marble, but the stalactite niche within its elongated, horseshoe-shaped surround and the side pilasters are essentially Anatolian, as is the geometric character of the star-shaped decorations of the lateral panels. Both its plan and many of its decorations bear a close resemblance to those of the Sivas-Kayseri Sultan Han.

16 The Mosque of Sultan 'Palas' Han on the Kayseri–Sivas Road, likewise a royal foundation, was begun in 1230 and completed ten years later. The mosque stands in the centre of the courtyard, rising most gracefully from a base formed of four horseshoe-shaped arches. Entrance to it

is gained by means of a double flight of steps which encircles the arch facing the entrance gate of the han.

17 Detail of the sculptured decoration on the face of one of the arches beneath the mosque of the Sivas-Kayseri Sultan Han. A strongly-Asiatic rendering of the spade or heart-shaped motif frames the arch; its line is repeated by a rather Celtic-style pattern of an interlocking type which is more characteristic of metal-work than of stone-work, but which recurs on other sections of this building. A characteristic rosette pattern set in a geometric background helps to carry the eye upward towards the mosque, as does the strongly Central-Asian treatment and stylization of the triangles.

18 Detail of a snake-like decoration from another arch at the base of the same mosque. The snake was recognized by the Seljuks as the emblem of Aesculapius, and as such it was often used by them. The rendering sculptured for the hospital founded at Cankırı in 1235 by the Atabeg Cemaleddin Ferruk, director in 1220 of the Hospitals of Sivas, was chosen by the new University of Istanbul as its crest. The Sultan Han version is one of the finest of its date.

19 The drum of the doubtless once conically-roofed dome marking the centre of the great hall in the Sivas-Kayseri Sultan Han, showing details of its window and interior decoration.

20 The caravanserai at Tercan, a building which, like the adjacent mausoleum, belongs to the turn of the 12th century. This large, rectangular han was originally windowless on the outside, where the uniformity of its walls was broken by the tall, pencil-pointed towers set along them at regular intervals. In shape they recall the free-standing towers of somewhat earlier date erected in northern Persia to serve as mortuary monuments.

21 A vaulted gallery in the han at Tercan. Its exceptional height enabled camel-caravans to use it, though separate stabling was also provided for the use of horses and mules. As in the Ulu Cami at Erzurum, there is a complete absence of sculptured decoration—a characteristic which often helps to distinguish Saltukid buildings from those for which the Seljuks were responsible. Notwithstanding the lack of ornamentations, the ingenuity of the han's plan, the excellence of its proportions and the superb quality of its masonry entitles it to rank with the finest caravanserais of the period.

22 A gallery in the Sivas-Kayseri Sultan Han showing the excellence of the proportions and the masonry, and hinting at the splendour of the loftier central aisle.

23 Tokat Bridge built in 1250 at the expense of the Pervane Hamid b Abdul Kassim, son of the Vizir al Tusi, and of the Emir Seifeddin, the facts being recorded in the inscription carved on the stone plinth marking the centre of the bridge. The bridge is still used regularly by all types of traffic.

24 The Mama Hatun Kümbet, Tercan, was built in 1192 by Muffadel the Cross-eyed of Ahlat for the Saltukid princess who came to the help of Saladin when heen countered difficulties in the Tercan area. The kümbet is of an unusually complex character. It consists of a circular outer wall and a central mausoleum. The wall is adorned with a very ornate portal which faces the han; the slender, tall and pointed lateral niches to some extent recall the towers set along the walls of the han.

25 The Çifte (double) or Hatuniye Medrese, Erzurum, built in 1253 by Huand Hatun, the daughter of Alaeddin Keykûbad II, is now used as a museum. Its entrance is topped by the two elaborately-tiled minarets from which it derives its name; they recall to some extent those of Sivas's slightly-later Çifte Medrese, plate 11. Within, the lateral porticoes, enclosing a rectangular courtyard, contain central ivan-shaped halls, each of which is flanked by six rooms disposed on two floors. The founder's mausoleum occupies the far end, the blind arcading on its conical roof repeating the movement of the broader arcades along its side walls. Many sections of the building are sculptured.

26 On the inside the round outer wall of the Mama Hatun Kümbet, Tercan, is divided into twelve shallow alcoves. Ten of these contain coffins, while that to the right of the door held a mihrab, and that to the left, the staircase leading to an uncovered walk along the top of the wall, the idea for which may have been derived from Sultan Sencer's two-storeyed brick mausoleum in Persia. At Tercan the centre of the enclosure is occupied by Mama Hatun's two-storeyed stone mausoleum, itself an eight-lobed structure with ribs separating its apse-shaped sections, the lines of which are recalled in the conical roof by a double-ribbed form of blind arcading. The princess's coffin still occupies the lower chamber, while a mihrab transforms the upper into a chapel.

27 The Eşrefoglu Mosque at Beyşehir was founded in 1296–98 by a family of that name which was to establish itself soon after the Seljuks' collapse as the rulers of a Beylik or principality bearing their name. Though the mosque is of a late date it is archaic in type, for it retains, together with the traditional outlines of its walls, minaret and türbe, the flat roof of the mosque which characterizes the opening phase of Seljukid architecture in Asia Minor.

28 Divriği castle, built in 1180/81 for the Seljuks' Menguçek vassal, contained a mosque built by Hasan b Pıruz of Maragha in Persia. The castle's massive bastions and walls presented a formidable deterrent to invaders of the period.

29 The Kızıl Kule or Red Tower formed the pivot of Alaiye's defences. Built of ashlar blocks in 1226 by the Syrian architect Abu Ali b Abi-r-Rakka all Kattani of Aleppo, it is an octagonal structure measuring 95 feet in diameter and 108 feet in height at its tallest point. The plan of its interior is singularly complicated (see fig. 20), each of its five storeys being different. Stone staircases connect the floors and lead to a roof terrace. For a detailed study see Seton Lloyd and D. Storm Rice, *Alanya*, London, 1958.

30 The front of the naval arsenal or Tersane at Alaiye, built in 1228, two years after the Kızıl Kule which so effectively protected it. From the outside all that is to be seen is the sea wall with its five horseshoe-shaped openings, and traces of its battlements. This measures 187 feet in length. The arches lead into five vaulted galleries which run back under the rock to a depth of 131 feet (see fig. 9). They are built of baked brick and lit by holes set at regular intervals in their roofs. The walls separating the galleries are broken by four arches and each gallery is so large that big ships could shelter or be built in secret within it. The structure is still used today by the local fishermen.

31 The kümbet of the seyit Mahmud Hairani, Akşehir, is dated to 1224. The transition from the square chamber to the conical roof is achieved by means of an octagonal base to a circular drum, the smoothness of which is broken by means of apse-shaped shafts.

32 The türbe of Nüreddin ibn Sentimur at Tokat is dated to 1313. In this late example the roof of the conical turret is broken up into triangular sections.

33 A drawing by Friar Rubruquis of the tents which he saw when he visited the Mongol court in 1253 is reproduced in de Bergeron's edition of his work. These tents may well have served as prototypes for the Seljukid mausolea.

34 The Döner Kümbet at Kayseri is dated to 1276. Though traditional in shape, it is distinguished by its extremely elaborate and spirited sculptured decorations. It was built for the Princess Shah Cıhan Hatun and is amongst the most ornate of its kind. Its decorations consist of arabesque and geometric compositions as well as of a number of animal forms such as lions, eagles and stylized birds, with palm leaves symbolizing the tree of life.

35 A mausoleum built in 1322 on the shore of Lake Van, midway between Van and Achtavan, at the order of Izzaldın for his wife, the Princess Halima. Only the shape of the blind arcading and the niches on the octagonal faces of its walls betray its late date.

36 The türbe of Hudavend Hatun, a daughter of Kılıçarslan IV, builder of the Alaeddin Kiosk at Konya (plate 2), was built at Nigde in 1312. Shaped as a septagon, this two-storeyed mausoleum has a richly-sculptured doorway, and its yellow limestone walls are topped with a harder stone enclosed within marble bands, which is likewise intricately carved. Its motifs include arabesques and animal forms, among which lions, stags and birds with human heads play a prominent part.

37 A column and capital from the portico of Çifte Medrese, Erzurum, 1253, showing the successful use of a geometric motif on the shaft and a floral composition on the capital.

38 The ruined mosque at Dunyaşır, the modern Koş Hisar, once an important halt for caravans. The ruin clearly displays the various building methods used by the Seljuks.

39 A detail from the north portal of the Ulu Cami, Divriği, built in 1228 by Ahmet, son of Ibrahim of Tiflis, and Khurramshah, son of Muhid of Ahlat. Many of its motifs recall Indian rather than Caucasian prototypes. The round medallion with its geometric background and central device may well have been inspired by a shield of an earlier date. Notice the delicacy of the sculptured inscription running along the top of the stalactite-shaped capital.

40 Another detail from the same portal, in which the crescent and floral patterns are treated in a manner which recalls Indian gold-filigree work.

41 Another detail from the same portal. Here the influences both of Central Asia and of Northern Persia prevail, the style recalling that of much of the stucco work at Hamadan, more particularly the decorations of the Gumbat-i-Alawiyan there.

42 A bronze handle in the form of a bull's head from the Koyunoglu collection in Konya, measuring 6 cm. by 6 cm.

43 Detail from the façade of Karatay Han, built in 1240/41 for the Vizir Celaleddin Karatay. Stars and geometric shapes are combined with arabesque motifs and a delicately executed, rather Persian-looking figure of a bird.

44 Detail from the façade of Ak Han, Aksaray, built between 1250 and 1260. The style in which the bird is rendered is very different from that of the Karatay Han sculpture; it is more direct, severe and heraldic in character. Here the geometric decoration is replaced by a basket-like interlacing formed of circles and curved bands. The triangular-shaped pattern of the edging is of Central-Asian character, and very similar to that which appears on the mosque of the Sivas-Kayseri Sultan Han, plate 17, and also on other sections of Ak Han, see fig. 13.

45 A sculpture of the sun from the façade of Ak Han, Aksaray. It resembles a rather less well-preserved carving from the façade of the Daruşşifa Hospital, Sivas, 1217, where it is accompanied by one of the moon.

46 Detail from the façade of the Turumtay mausoleum, Amasya, dated to 1278/79. This two-storeyed monument contains the embalmed remains of Seifeddin Turumtay, Emir of Amasya. The upper sections of its walls are decorated with panels or bands of varying sizes containing repeat patterns.

47 A bronze weight of Ortokid workmanship from the Bibliothèque Nationale, Paris. The Royal Scottish Museum, Edinburgh, possesses a very similar example. In both the prevailing influence is Persian, but the markings on the bodies of the human-headed gryphons are to be found on many beasts of Anatolian character and of Seljukid workmanship.

48 A bronze weight from the Koyunoglu collection in Konya measuring 12 cm. in diameter. Its simple decoration of star and floral shapes is typically Seljukid.

49 A lion from the citadel at Divriği. Though the castle dates from 1180/81, one of the citadel gates bears the date of 1236, and the other 1242; the sculpture is more likely to fall between the latter dates than the first two. The treatment of the lion has an affinity with certain Scythian bone carvings, as for example the head of the 7th to 6th century B.C. from Kelermes, reproduced on plate 35 of *The Scythians*, T. Talbot Rice, London, 1957.

50 A free-standing stone sculpture of a lion, from the Alaeddin Kiosk, Konya, and thus dating from between 1246 and 1264. It is now preserved in the Museum of Turkish and Islamic Art at Istanbul. It is 1·56 m. high, and is closer to a Hittite than a Scythian prototype.

51 A free-standing stone sculpture of a sphinx measuring 58 cm. in height and 78 cm. in length. It is of 13th-century date and is now preserved in the Museum of Turkish and Islamic Art at Istanbul. Sculptures in the round were comparatively rare in the Seljukid period and were generally confined to representations of lions. Though mutilated, the face of the sphinx is very expressive.

52 A sculptured panel from the façade of Çifte Medrese, Erzurum, 1253, showing two lions standing on either side of the tree of life with an eagle above it. The composition is set in a horseshoe-shaped arch, and ornamented bosses complete the design.

53 A double-headed eagle from the façade of the mental hospital at Divriği, 1228. Of heraldic conception, its technique is closer to the metal worker's than the sculptor's, for there is an element of the jeweller's art in the elongation of the bird's legs, the stylization of its tail and the crescent-shaped device separating its body from its tail.

54 A sculptured slab displaying an eagle, from the citadel at Konya, and thus to be dated to about the year 1221. It measures 90 cm. by 94 cm., and is preserved in the Ince Minare Museum, Konya. It was originally placed above the two winged genii set over the main entrance to the citadel, and resembles in style the eagle on the contemporary brocade shown on plate 78.

55 A double-headed eagle from the façade of Çifte Medrese, Erzurum, 1253, a variant of that illustrated on plate 52.

56 A window-surround which Van Berchem and Strzygowski associate with Dıyarbakır, now preserved in the Museum of Turkish and Islamic Art in Istanbul. A Kufic inscription, scrolls and triangles form the basic motifs, but heraldic beasts enliven the design. The scholars referred to above are of the opinion, in *Amida*, Heidelberg, 1910, p. 357, that its inscription is devoid of historical interest and that the sculpture belongs to the 12th century, but the similarity in the treatment of the wings on the lion-like creatures and that of a creature from Konya's citadel (see fig. 45) makes a date at the beginning of the 13th century seem more likely. This view finds further support when the hawks on this sculpture are compared with that on the façade of Aksaray's Ak Han, shown on plate 44.

57 This sculpture of a dragon with a snake's body and a tail terminating in another dragon's head once adorned the wall of Konya's citadel, and is thus to be dated to about the year 1221. It measures 33 cm. by 96 cm. and resembles similar beasts of the same date which formerly adorned the Talisman Gate at Baghdad, where they were shown being strangled by the Caliph Nasir because they represented his enemies, the Shah of Kwarazm and the Mongol invaders. Though the dragon form in art could have reached the Seljuks equally well from China as from the Christian world, it may well have been indigenous, for Firdausi used it as the symbol of the Central-Asian nomad of Turkish origin.

58 A sculptured slab from Konya's citadel, 50 cm. by 55 cm., dating from about 1221, now preserved in the Ince Minare Museum, Konya. It shows a man seated on a camp stool holding a hawk on his gloved right hand as he touches the chin of a smaller figure with his left. His beard and moustache are carefully trimmed and his clothes are more elaborate than those shown on other sculptures of this type; this feature, together with the elderly appearance of the smaller figure, seems to suggest that the sculpture represents a sultan and one of his subjects rather than a man and child. The treatment of the carving is not unlike that on a funerary monument of the classical period and may well have been inspired by an early work of the latter type.

59 Sculptured slab showing an elephant being pursued by a wild beast. It was built into the wall of Konya's citadel and thus dates from about

the year 1221. It measures 1·50 m. by 55 cm. and is preserved in the Ince Minare Museum, Konya. Sarre in his *Kleinasiatischer Kleinkunst* compares the elephant on this slab to that on the elephant cloth from Charle﹣magne's tomb at Achen and suggests that the artists who created these elephants were influenced by a Sasanian textile. However, direct contact with India via Ghazna or Kwarazm can equally well account for the resemblance, especially since the dot﹣and﹣comma markings on the body of the pursuing monster have in this instance assumed shapes that often appear in Indian jewellery.

60   A sculptured stone measuring 50 cm. by 57 cm. from the walls of Konya's citadel, and thus dating from about the year 1221, now pre﹣served in the Ince Minare Museum at Konya. It shows a man seated cross﹣legged, holding a round object in one hand. The object has been described as an apple but comparison with Sasanian representations of this scene suggest that it should in fact be a drinking﹣cup; by the 13th century the original meaning of the scene had been forgotten, and Seljukid sculptors continued to depict it without understanding its significance.

61   A stone measuring 90 cm. by 90 cm., showing two soldiers wearing pointed helms and chain﹣mail jerkins, of 13th﹣century date. The armour appears to conform with Firdausi's description of Turkish equipment which, he said, was black in colour. The style of the sculpture is coarse and primitive, but not unlike that of a rather more Uygur rendering of two figures ascribed to Seljukid workmanship, now belonging to a private collection in America, but reproduced in fig. 376 of E. Diez and Oktay Aslanapa, *Türk Sanatı*. The Anatolian sculpture is to be seen in the Museum of Turkish and Islamic Art, Istanbul.

62   One of a pair of stone sculptured figures, measuring 153 cm. by 94 cm., which were originally placed above the main entrance to the citadel at Konya and which are therefore to be dated to about the year 1221. They are now preserved in the Ince Minare Museum at Konya. Considered by Texier to represent Ormuzd and Ariman, that is, Good and Evil, they equally vividly recall many classical and Byzantine figures of winged victories and angels, as well as the Sasanian genii which Chosro I erected in A.D. 620 at Taq﹣i﹣bustan. The crowns worn by the Konya figures closely resemble that of the Caliph Nasir as shown on the sculp﹣ture set above the entrance to Baghdad's Talisman Gate in 1222, and

unfortunately blown up in 1917 when the tower was used as a munitions dump. The Konya figures held towels in their left hands and possibly also a round object, which may have represented the sun and moon or the world.

63 Sculpture showing a seated lute-player, a 13th-century work now in the Staatliches Museen, Berlin. Though simple in presentation, in this instance the workmanship is of high quality, and the sculpture is subtle, sensitive and beautiful. The Seljuks delighted in music, and their artists, and more especially their potters, were fond of depicting lute-players. A tile from the palace at Kubadabad, now in the Karatay Museum at Konya, shows a rather more Persian type of treatment of the subject than does this sculpture.

64 A bronze and enamel dish bearing the name of the Ortokid Prince Sukman ibn Daud of Hisn-Kaifa, who reigned from 1114 to 1144. Its shape and also the style of some of its superb enamels, more especially of the larger central figure, are strongly Byzantine and suggest Greek workmanship, but some of the smaller animal motifs are akin to the embroidered medallions on Thomas à Becket's cope, which is preserved at Fermo and which Professor Storm Rice identifies as of Muslim origin. Yet even if the dish were made by a Greek, as seems probable, it must nevertheless have been produced in a Muslim workshop, and it cannot in its day have been unique.

65 Gold belt buckle measuring 7·5 cm. by 6 cm. now in the Islamic Department of the Berlin Museum, West. The creatures on it are presented in the forthright manner which belies the superficial Persian appearance of the buckle, and stamps it as an Anatolian work. The beasts' leaf-shaped wings and the eagles' heads resemble various designs of 13th-century date, but their strong similarity to a pair of crowned griffins executed in stucco and preserved in the museum at Etchmiadzin suggests a link with Keyhüsrev II when, because of his devotion to his Georgian wife, Caucasian influence was to the fore. Thus a date between 1236 and 1246 may well be a likely one for this buckle.

66 The doors of the carved wooden pulpit from the Eşrefoglu Mosque at Beyşehir should be assigned to the 13th century. The sides of the pulpit are carved with equally spirited geometric designs.

67 A 13th-century carved wooden door in which geometric patterns, floral designs and arabesques are extremely well combined with script to form a harmonious decoration.

68 Wooden shutters from the mosque of Hakim Bey, Konya, 1258. The carving is executed with great delicacy, and the intricate design evolves with the grace and elegance which distinguishes the best work.

69 The tiled mihrab from the Sahip Ata Medrese, Konya, founded by the Vizir in 1258 and built for him by Kelük b Abdulla, is a fine example of its kind. The technique of glazed tile mosaic work necessitated cutting the tiles into shaped sections which were curved on the inner side to ensure an exact fit.

70 One of the eight Seljukid carpets of 13th-century date which were discovered still in use in the Alaeddin Mosque in Konya early in this century. Now in the Mevlana Museum, Konya. Though damaged, this rug survives in practically its original dimensions, measuring about three metres in width. Professor K. Erdman provides good reason, in his booklet on *Der Türkische Teppich des 15 Jahrhunderts*, Istanbul, for ascribing the carpet to a Konya workshop and for thinking that it was presented to the mosque, if not by the Sultan, as seems very probable, then at any rate by one of his foremost ministers, or courtiers.

71 This carved and painted Koran stand made of nut wood was presented to Celaleddin Rumi in 1278/79 by Cemaleddin as Sahıbı and is now preserved in the Mevlana Museum, Konya. It measures 94·5 cm. by 42·5 cm. The exterior of the stand is exquisitely carved with elaborate arabesques enclosed in a square border, the inscription cut along the top of the lower section being executed with particular skill and elegance.

72 Detail of the painted decoration on an inner side of the Koran stand. This panel provides us with what is still an unique example of Seljukid painting. The decoration is carried out in gold and black on a red ground. The main design is enclosed in a circle set in a square border, the empty spaces at the corners being filled in with elaborate palmette patterns. The medallion contains as its central motif a strongly-stylized double-headed eagle measuring 35 cm. in length, presented amidst a web-like background of repeat floral arabesques through which, as in a jungle, appear fourteen lions. To judge by descriptions the painted beams in the

Alaeddin Kiosk at Konya, which were but ten to twenty years earlier in date, must have been very similar in style, and since this painting has unmistakable affinities with those of the Palazzo Reale at Palermo, it is to the Saracenic paintings of Sicily that we should perhaps look to gain some idea of what the Seljukid paintings of Konya may have been like.

73 The Koran stand shown fully-opened with the painted sides ready to support the Koran and the carved backs hidden from view.

74 A somewhat coarse bowl intended for everyday use, from the Kayseri Museum. It measures 16·5 cm. in diameter and is to be dated to the mid-13th century. On the outside its green ground carries brown stripes; inside, the brown design is set against a yellow ground and given a green overglaze. The shield-shaped central motif contains a floral emblem.

75 A tile showing Bahram Gur and Leila hunting, 20 cm. square. It probably came originally from the Alaeddin Palace at Konya and is now in the Koyunoglu collection there. Though Uygur and Persian elements are to the fore, the style and design are basically Anatolian, and so are both the paste and the colour-scheme. The prevailing colour is blue; it has a greenish tinge in the background, a whitish one in the horse and a touch of purple in the hare. The blue saddle-cloth contrasts with Bahram Gur's clothes, which vary from purple to mid-blue and are touched with gold, as are Leila's pale green garments. There are also some touches of black.

76 A large fragment of a small mid-13th-century Seljukid carpet from the Alaeddin Mosque at Konya, now preserved in the Mevlana Museum at Konya. The diamond-shaped lozenges contain a motif derived from an earlier design showing animals set back to back (see figs. 54 a and b). At regular intervals a shield- or heart-shaped pattern of a characteristic type intrudes on the basic design.

77 Part of a red and gold brocade found in an abbey in the Auvergne and now preserved in the Musée Historique des Tissus, Lyons. The inscrip-tion forming the border bears the date of 616 H., that is to say A.D.1218/19, and refers to the Sultan Keykûbad I, son of Sultan Keyhüsrev, the builder of much of Konya. Though less popular than lions, leopards were also used to symbolize royal power; those shown on the textile hold their bodies sideways but their faces are shown frontally, while their claws clutch at a form which resembles that of the snake intertwined in the claws of an eagle on a sculpture from Konya's citadel. The 1929 edition

of the Lyons Museum's catalogue suggests that the brocade was made in Egypt, but there is no valid reason for thinking so, as the style of the drawing and all the elements in the design are characteristically Anatolian. Parallels for most of them can be found in the tiles made for Konya's palace as well as in the sculptures.

78 Fragment of a gold and red brocade from the Apollinari shrine in Siegburg, belonging to the Islamic Department of the museum in West Berlin. Though the textile has been ascribed both to Palermo and to Baghdad it is typical of the Seljuks of Asia Minor, and must surely have been made in Konya for a sultan or an important member of his court. Eagles, an emblem of royalty, form its main motif; in style they are reminiscent of the sculptured eagle holding a serpent in its claws which, in Laborde's sketch dated to 1825, (see plate 10), appears above an entrance to the citadel. As such the textile is probably to be associated with Alaeddin Keykûbad I (1219–1235) or his immediate successor, and it is sad that no trace of its border, which might well have contained an inscription, has been preserved. The shield-like shape of the medallion might seem to be of western origin, yet the shape occurs quite frequently in Islamic art. Mayer in his work on Saracenic heraldry thinks that it represented an emblem of office, though it cannot be identified today. The device appears again on the bowl from the museum at Kayseri shown on plate 74.

79 Obverse of a selection of Seljukid coins, natural size. From left to right these are:
Top row: Silver coin of Kılıçarslan II, Konya, 582 H., A.D. 1186; silver coin of Mesud II, Mardin-Baiburt, 687–89 H., A.D. 1287–89; silver coin of Keyhüsrev III, Konya, 674 H., A.D. 1275.
Middle row: Silver coin of Kılıçarslan IV, Sivas, 646 H., A.D. 1248; silver coin of Keyhüsrev II, Sivas, 638 H., A.D. 1240; silver coin of Keykâvus I, Konya 610 H., A.D. 1212; silver coin of Keyhüsrev I, Konya 604 H., A.D. 1205.
Bottom row: Silver coin of Süleyman II, Kayseri, 597 H., A.D. 1201; copper coin of Süleyman II, no date or mint mark; copper coin of Mûgisûddin Tugrul Shah, 613 H., A.D. 1215; silver coin of Keykâvus I, Konya, 610 H., A.D. 1212.

80 Seljukid coins as listed above (plate 79), showing reverses.

Index

Q